Kids
Ending Hunger:
What Can WE Do?

A Get-into-Action Book for Kids
and
Their Parents and Teachers

Tracy Apple Howard
with Sage Alexandra Howard

Andrews and McMeel
A Universal Press Syndicate Company
Kansas City

Illustrations by Renee Walas Deprey and Elizabeth Morales-Denney

Library of Congress Cataloging-in-Publication Data

Howard, Tracy Apple.
    Kids Ending Hunger: what can we do?: a get-into-action book for kids and their parents and teachers / Tracy Apple Howard with Sage Alexandra Howard.
        p. cm.
    Includes bibliographical references.
    Summary: Discusses hunger in the world and presents activities children and their families can engage in to alleviate it.
    ISBN 0-8362-7000-2
    1. Food relief—Juvenile literature.   2. Children—Nutrition— Juvenile literature.   [1. Hunger.   2. Food relief.]   I. Howard, Sage Alexandra.   II. Title.
HV696.F6H68   1992
363.8'83—dc20   92-18718
                                                         CIP
                                                         AC

92   93   94   95   96   10   9   8   7   6   5   4   3   2   1

This book is dedicated to the children of the world—

Those who suffer and die of hunger, needlessly;

And those who would like to do something about it.

What's in the Book

About Kids Ending Hunger—Is It Possible?...........1

Can hunger really be ended? . . . what ending hunger
has to do with saving the earth

The Problem—How Bad Is It? 9

What is hunger? . . . the power of words . . . how much
is a billion? . . . where are the hungry people? . . . the
World Summit for Children . . . a story about some kids
in Africa . . . two kinds of hunger: famine, chronic
hunger

About the Solutions—Can We End It? 49

A story about some kids in India . . . the Child
Survival Campaign . . . a sad story about the African
kids . . . a happier story about the Indian kids . . .
how much it would cost to end hunger . . . how
hunger organizations help . . . a story about a hungry
family in North America . . . how GOBI is saving kids'
lives . . . a story about a class of kids in North America
who decide to do something to help

50 Things Kids Can Do to End Hunger......107

Kinds of things you can do . . . activities you and your friends and family can do

Kids Ending Hunger— What Does It Really Matter?......151

What's so good about ending hunger anyway? . . . the big question

Resources—How Can I Find Out More?......157

People and groups that can help . . . resources for teachers and parents . . . audiovisual materials . . . books for kids . . . magazines . . . an ending-hunger calendar

About the Information in This Book......185

References . . . permissions . . . special ending-hunger words

Afterword and Acknowledgments......191

Messages from the authors . . . one more thing . . . tribute . . . acknowledgments

About Kids Ending Hunger– Is It Possible?

Message to Kids

You're going to find out a lot about hunger—and ending it—in this book.

The section called "50 Things Kids Can Do to End Hunger" is loaded with ideas about what you can actually **do**.

As you're going through the book, if you get impatient and want to jump into action, it's fine to skip to that section and get started.

You don't need to go in order or wait for anything!

Message to Parents and Teachers

Children are profoundly interested in the fate of other children. When given the opportunity to really make a difference with a global issue such as ending hunger, like many of the rest of us they leap at the chance.

The children who have interacted with this book so far have had a lot to say, a lot to ask. We hope you will find in these pages the information you need to answer their questions—the ones that are answerable, of course. To the other questions, such as "How come we let all those kids die of hunger?", you will need to search your own soul for an answer that can be given to children who look to you to represent what is good and right in life.

As **parents** we have the inexpressible joy of being able to watch our children develop and grow into full human beings, unlike the tens of thousands of our counterparts around the world who daily must bury children they love.

As **teachers** we help children discover themselves and what matters—and how to build the kind of world we all want to live in. If the teachers and students of the world were to unite around the issue of ending hunger, if they made it their own personal challenge and goal, history would be altered—and the lives of millions of children saved. It is a challenge appropriate to these times and to this generation of children.

May our children lead us in eliminating the ravages of hunger in our time, and may our own humanity and vision be restored as well.

Ending Hunger Is Possible!

This book is about the children who died yesterday of hunger, and the millions of others who went to bed hungry.

It is also about you, your friends, and other kids like you around the world who want to do something about it.

We are alive at a very great time. For the first time in the history of the world, it is possible to feed the whole human family. For the first time in the history of the world, the leaders of almost every country on earth have agreed to work toward ending hunger, and children no longer need to die of hunger.

Ending hunger on this planet is possible. It will take plenty of work, money, and commitment to make it happen. But it is possible!

It will take people saying: "The time has come to end hunger, once and for all! Let's do it! Let's do whatever it takes to make it happen! No more hunger in our world!"

Some people would ask: "Why are you talking to children about this problem? Kids are interested in themselves. They're too young to care about what is happening to the world's children. They're too young to help."

We don't think that's true about you.

Sure, you want to play and have fun and have a great life—we all do. But we have the idea that you also want that for **all** children. Our guess is that a world without hunger is your dream, too.

And we hope that you will find in your heart, and in your spirit, the courage to stand up for the world's children, to let them into your heart, to stand with and for them, and to help make something happen that has never been done by any people before: **end hunger on our planet.**

What can kids do? Well, that's what this book is about.

Sage, who is nine, and her mother, Tracy, wrote this book to let you know about hunger and the hungry people in our world, and to let you know some things that you and your parents, or brothers and sisters, or cousins, or friends, or some of the kids and teachers in your school, or even your whole school can do to end hunger.

And when the time comes that you read in the newspaper or hear on TV that hunger has been ended, that children no longer suffer from hunger or famine—when that time comes, you will have the great joy and satisfaction of knowing that you were one of the people who made it happen.

What a great gift, what a great accomplishment—for you, and for the children of the world.

Tracy and Sage Howard
Yamanakako, Japan

What's Ending Hunger Got to Do with

When you talk to people about ending world hunger, some of them may say to you:

"I am interested in saving the earth."

"I am interested in recycling."

"I want to end pollution."

"I don't have time to get involved in ending world hunger."

Others might say:

"Peace is more important."

"I'm into world peace."

"I don't have time to get involved in ending hunger."

Here is what you can point out to them:

We have only one earth. In many parts of the world there are people who are not being careful about the earth's resources because they are dying from hunger.

They cut down trees because they need fuel to cook their food. They farm on land that is worn out because they have no other place to grow their food.

They cannot pay attention to saving the earth because they are trying their best just to stay alive.

Hungry people have extra-large families to help them survive, too. When hunger is ended and mothers know that their babies will not die of hunger or disease, they begin to have fewer children. And that's good for the earth.

Saving the Earth?

If we want to get the hungry people on the "Save the Earth" team, then we first need to help them take care of their basic needs. Then they, too, will be able to care for the earth.

You could also mention that human beings are one of the earth's greatest resources, but 13 million to 18 million of these precious resources die from hunger each year.

To your friends who want world peace, you could say that you do, too. You could tell them that wars are less frequent when all people have a chance to feed themselves and their families. They might be surprised to find out that the number of people who die of hunger **every three and a half days** is the same as all the people who died from the atomic bomb that was exploded over Hiroshima during World War II.

Ending hunger is an important achievement for a world that wants peace.

The Problem–
How Bad Is It?

What is hunger, anyway?

What you feel when you skip lunch, or when supper is an hour late?

Not really.

That's not what we mean when we talk about hunger in this book. We would call that **appetite**.

Maybe your stomach rumbles, or hurts, or you feel grumpy. Still, that is not what we mean when we talk about hunger.

Hunger is when a person does not get enough food to be healthy. Even if people get enough food to feel full, if the food they are eating will not keep them healthy, will not make their bodies strong, we call it hunger.

This kind of hunger doesn't just hurt. It kills.

Mostly it kills children. They are the ones who get weak and die when their bodies are not properly fed.

Every day while many of us enjoy having a home, food to eat, and time to play, 600 million—that's 600,000,000—children are hungry.

Thousands upon thousands of them die. Every day.

Kids your age, many younger.

Many, many more live their whole lives with hunger—not food—in their bellies.

Their bodies never get a chance to grow strong.

What can we do? Feel guilty that we have so much?

Feeling guilty doesn't help.

How about **doing** something about it?

How could we do anything?

10

Would you like to?

Of course you would. You are a human being with a heart. You care. So do other kids.

Ask someone in your family to read these two pages to you—slowly—to get a better idea of what life would be like if you and your family were hungry. Close your eyes and imagine.

Think about your house. Picture it in your mind, both inside and outside. Now pretend to do these things:

- Shut off the electricity, and take away everything that uses it: lights, TV, clock radio, stove, stereo, toaster, refrigerator, washing machine.

- Now shut off the heat if it's winter, or the air conditioning if it's summer.

- Now shut off the running water.

- Take out the beds, chairs, rugs, curtains. Take it all out except for a few old blankets, a kitchen table, and one chair. Your family will sleep on the floor from now on. The clocks are gone, but you don't need them because you wake up before sunrise and go to bed when it gets dark most evenings.

- Get rid of all the extra clothing. You and everyone in your family are left with only your oldest outfit. The only person who may keep a pair of shoes is the head of your family.

- Get rid of all the books, newspapers, and magazines. Your family can't use them anyway, because none of you can read.

- Now go to the kitchen and look in the cupboards. A box of matches, a small bag of flour, some sugar and salt, a few onions, and a dish of beans may stay. Take away all the rest—the fresh fruit and vegetables, the packages of food, the canned food, the meat, the milk, the snack food. Your house is an empty shell.

And now, your house itself is gone.

- Move your family into a one-room shack. Your grandparents and uncle and aunt and cousin move in, too. Your little shed is crowded, but you are better off than many, for you have a roof over your head.

- Remove all the other houses in your neighborhood and replace them with shacks like yours. Tear up any paved streets or sidewalks. There are no trees—they were needed for firewood.

- Send the special helpers away from your community. No more mail, no more firefighters. There is a school three miles away in a small, empty building. Only a few of the kids on your street go—the rest work. There are no hospitals nearby. The nearest doctor is 10 miles away. You can get there by bicycle if your family has one. Or you can go by bus—there is usually room on top, if not inside. If someone in your family gets sick, there are midwives and medicine men and herbs and charms and prayers.

In your whole little town there is only one radio.

Most of the time you are tired. When there is work, you and your parents must work hard, with almost no stopping, all day long. Even the littlest children help. They go to get water and wood, and they take care of the landowner's animals and the crops. The farmland is worn out, but there is no other place to grow food.

When there is no work, you and your family are always trying to find some, or trying to find some food, maybe something that someone else has thrown out. Today there is just enough food to feed your family.

This is the life that poor and hungry children and their parents live. Every day, every month, every year.

Okay, you can open your eyes now.

Excerpted and modified from Robert Heilbroner, *The Great Ascent* (Harper & Row, 1983).

You and other kids can actually make a big difference in ending hunger.

How can you help? What can you do?

The first thing you can do, something that amazingly few people have really done, is to let the hungry people in. Not into your house or your town—into your heart. Into your thoughts. Into your dreams. Into your hopes. Into your plans for the future.

This doesn't mean to feel sorry for them, or feel bad for them. It means to know about them, and understand that they are fine, hardworking people who deserve a better chance in life.

To do that it will help to realize that the hungry people, the hungry children of the world are very, very much like you—except that they don't have enough to eat, and they get sick more. (If you have traveled to a country where there is a lot of hunger, you probably know that already.) But they laugh, they play and tease, they look at sunsets, they giggle, they like to smell good things cooking, they love their parents and playing with their friends . . .

The difference is that they were born into a situation where their family cannot get enough food to feed them.

Once you have opened yourself up to the hungry people of the world, there are two main ways you can help end hunger: through your **actions** and through your **words**.

Words.

You see them on this page, you speak them all day long.

But do you really know how powerful they are?

Do you know what a difference **talking** can make?

One of the most important actions you can take in ending hunger is to tell other people about the problem, tell them that ending hunger is possible, and ask them to get involved and take action themselves.

Because when enough people want to end it, and know it is possible—when enough people get involved, and commit themselves to ending it—we will be able to end hunger.

One reason people may not be involved is that many parents—maybe even yours—don't know how many people suffer and die from hunger every day, and how many of them are kids.

They also may not know that it is now possible to **end** world hunger altogether. (When **they** were kids, it simply wasn't possible to feed everyone. But now it is.)

They don't know that recently the leaders of almost every country on earth made a promise that by the year 2000 they will end the hunger of the kids in their countries.

My parents were young an awfully long time ago. Practically the dark ages. I think they forgot everything they learned at school anyway.

My daddy knows everything.

How can we get people involved?

You know how to get someone's attention if you really need it, right? If you saw a house on fire and you knew there were kids trapped inside, you'd get adults to listen to you—fast.

Well, **40,000 children died yesterday**—and today—of hunger and diseases that could have been prevented. **Millions** more are hungry.

That is certainly worth speaking up about, wouldn't you say?

And yet, somehow we don't hear about it.

We don't read about it in the newspapers.

It isn't on TV.

Why do you suppose that is?

Here's one way to get people's attention. Write the words "40,000 KIDS DIED OF HUNGER TODAY" with a wide black pen or crayon on a strip of paper two inches wide. Tape the strip on top of a newspaper headline, covering the headline that is there. Put your newspaper where other people will see it at home, or show it to your class at school.

When people ask you about it, be sure to mention that that headline would appear not just today, not just tomorrow, but day after day after day.

There Is Enough

There is already enough food to feed everyone! There is enough grain (food like rice, and wheat for bread) to feed all the people on earth, plus all the people who will be born in the next 10 years.

Of course, we wouldn't want to eat just bread. But still, it's good to know there is plenty of food to go around.

Can kids be heroes?

Can kids lead the way in ending hunger?

Absolutely!

And you can begin by speaking up!

You can let your friends, your family, teachers, and other people know it is not all right with you that millions of children get sick and even die from hunger, and you can let them know that you intend to do something about it.

Kids Making a Difference

Children can be heroes and lead the way for other children—and for adults. It has happened before!

In 1990, a boy named Trevor saw a story on homelessness in Philadelphia on the TV news and asked his father if they could take the man in the story a blanket. Then he wanted to go back and take more blankets and food, for the others. He asked other people to contribute things, and delivered them as well. People heard about Trevor on TV and in the newspapers, and they wanted to help, too. Now there is a Trevor Foundation helping to end hunger and homelessness in Philadelphia.

That same year, a 7-year-old boy in England named Eli was worried about the people in Ethiopia, Africa, who were in danger of starving because of a famine caused by the war there. He decided to write to then–Soviet President Gorbachev and ask him to help end the war in Ethiopia. He told his friends about the project, and they told their friends, and they all decided to start a letter-writing campaign. Then newspapers and TV reporters told about his project. In the end Eli and a group of kids from 10 countries went to the Soviet Union and delivered 65,353 letters to Mrs. Gorbachev, the president's wife.

In 1983, a 10-year-old girl from Maine named Samantha Smith was afraid that the Soviet Union and the United States of America might have a war. She wrote a letter to the Russian leader at the time, Yuri Andropov, asking him why he wanted to hurt her country. Mr. Andropov wrote back, telling her he only wanted peace, and he invited her to come to the Soviet Union to talk with him and meet the people of the Soviet Union (Russia). So she did. After her trip she traveled all over the U.S., letting people know how friendly the Russian people were to her. She became a symbol of the United States's longing for peace, as well as the power of one person to make a difference. (Have you noticed there has been no war between the Soviet Union and the United States?!)

Anne Frank, a 12-year-old Jewish girl in Holland during World War II, kept a diary about her life in hiding for two years. In it she wrote that in spite of the horrible things that were happening in the war, she still believed that people are good at heart. When the Nazis discovered her family's hideout, she was taken and killed. Her journal was found and has been published in many different languages, inspiring people everywhere.

Sadako was a Japanese girl who was in Hiroshima the day the atom bomb was dropped, in 1945. Ten years later, at the age of 12, she died of leukemia, from the bomb's radiation. Before her death, she tried to make a thousand paper cranes in the hope that these good-luck symbols would keep her alive. She got to almost 700 before she died. Now all over the world, 1,000 origami cranes is a symbol for peace, and her statue stands in the Hiroshima Peace Garden.

In 1990, three Japanese junior high school students made sure that the prime minister at the time, Toshiki Kaifu, knew that the people of Japan wanted hunger to end and wanted him to attend an important summit of world leaders about ending hunger: They collected 16,255 signatures from kids and adults in Japan, and made an appointment to give all the signatures to the prime minister. You know what? Mr. Kaifu decided to meet with the kids and hear what they had to say—and he attended the summit.

That summer, a group of 75 Youth Ending Hunger students from 10 countries rode their bicycles 3,000 miles across the United States to make people aware that 40,000 kids die of hunger and easily preventable diseases every day. Lots of newspapers and TV stations covered the cyclists as they rode through their towns. By the end of the tour, more than 100 million people had heard about the ride and about what they could do to help end hunger.

During World War II, when the Nazis invaded Scandinavia, the children of Finland, Norway, and Denmark were determined to stand up to the soldiers—without getting themselves killed. They decided that kids throughout their countries would wear little red caps (like Santa's elves wear) to show that they were against the Nazis. When the Nazis found out, they made a law against wearing little red caps. So the children decided to wear paper clips instead. The Nazis didn't like that any better, and made it against the law to wear paper clips! Throughout the war, brave children carried messages, distributed pamphlets, and found ways to show that they, too, were unwilling to let the Nazis carry on with their cruelty.

When people know the facts, they get involved.

What can we tell people about ending hunger?

What are the facts?

Important Things to Tell Kids and Adults

■ A lot of people are suffering from hunger. Most of them are kids.

■ Forty thousand children die every single day. Most of those deaths are from hunger or sickness that could have been prevented.

■ More people have died of hunger in the last 5 years than have died in all the wars, revolutions, and murders in the last 150 years.

■ One out of every five people on this planet lives with the pain and sickness of hunger. That comes to almost a billion people. And most of them are children.

■ There are ways to end hunger. Over half the countries of the world have already done it! If the whole human family took on ending hunger, we could do it.

■ When hunger ends in a country, the population gets smaller, not bigger!

■ By ending hunger, we help save the environment. People whose families are not hungry can afford to take care of the earth's precious resources.

■ Hungry people are the ones who most want hunger to end. They are courageous and strong, and are working very, very hard to end their own hunger. It takes more courage for them to live their lives—even the children—than most of the rest of us will ever need to call upon in ours.

■ To end hunger, hungry people need food, but they also need something besides food. (On page 50 you will find out what that is.)

Learning the facts, and telling them to the kids and adults you know, can make a difference in ending hunger. No kidding!

In the "50 Things Kids Can Do to End Hunger" section you'll find a lot of ideas of how to share this information with other people.

What Happens When We Get Other People Involved?

Let's say you really want to end hunger. You read this book, you get some ideas, you do them. Great. But . . .

Let's say that one of the things you decide to do is to tell other people about hunger, so that they get involved, too.

Then **they** get all excited and get into action doing **their** ideas, also.

Pretty soon you've got 5, 10, 30, a hundred more people all working on ending hunger, all because of you.

You just got multiplied!

I don't get it.

Elementary, my dear Watson. If you just do something, that's one thing, but if you talk a bunch of other people into doing stuff, then tons more gets done. Anybody could figure that out.

If you know anybody like a radio announcer or a writer or minister or the head of some big group or organization or someone else who reaches lots of people, it would be great to give them this information. They could really spread the word about ending hunger!

How Much Is a Billion?

Close to 1 billion people are hungry. How much is a billion, anyway?

To count from one to a billion:

If you started today, and didn't stop all day or all night, TO GET TO A BILLION, IT WOULD TAKE YOU 62 YEARS! (How old would you be when you finished?)

Another way to do it is:

How did they figure that out? Can we try it?

Sure, weirdo. Let's go buy a billion M&Ms . . .

Imagine your classroom at school filled to the very top with M&Ms. Then imagine another classroom, also filled to the top with M&Ms. Then imagine one more classroom, filled one third of the way with M&Ms. The number of M&Ms you'd need for that project is . . . a billion.

Here's one more example:

If 1 billion kids climbed onto one another's shoulders, they would make a tower that reached all the way to the moon, and then came back to earth—and then went back to the moon again . . .

How did we figure these out?

Well, 27,648 M&Ms fit in a box the size of a large shoe box (one cubic foot). From there we multiplied to get the answer.

How did we figure how long it would take to count to a billion?

Well, Uncle Allan started counting 62 years ago . . .

Just kidding!

We multiplied again.

We figured it out by counting two seconds for each number. From there we multiplied.

And the tower of kids?

We figured an average of 4 feet for the height of kids from their toes to their shoulders (remember, they are standing on one another's shoulders), and multiplied by a billion. We divided that number by 5,280, which is the number of feet in a mile, and that came to 757,575 miles. Since the moon is about 239,000 miles from the earth, the tower would actually go to the moon and back about three times.

On the next page you'll see a map of the world with certain countries shaded in. We've colored in the "hungry" countries.

Every country in the world has **some** hungry people. Some countries have a lot.

Many experts feel that the **infant mortality rate** is one of the best ways to measure hunger in a country.

How Does the Infant Mortality Rate Work?

The infant mortality rate (IMR) keeps track of the number of babies who die before they are one year old.

For example, if 50 out of every thousand babies die before their first birthday, we say that country has an infant mortality rate of 50.

Experts say that if the IMR is higher than 50, it means that that country is having a real problem with hunger.

An infant mortality rate lower than 50 usually means that hunger is not the big killer in that country.

Every country in the world has some hungry people. Some countries have a lot.

Many experts feel that the infant mortality rate is one of the best ways to measure hunger in a country.

On the map on pages 28–29 we have shaded in the countries that have an infant mortality rate of 50 or more to show where the hungry people are.

Remember: Most of those hungry people are kids.

Where Do the Hungry People Live?

Countries with an infant mortality rate of 50 or above are shaded.

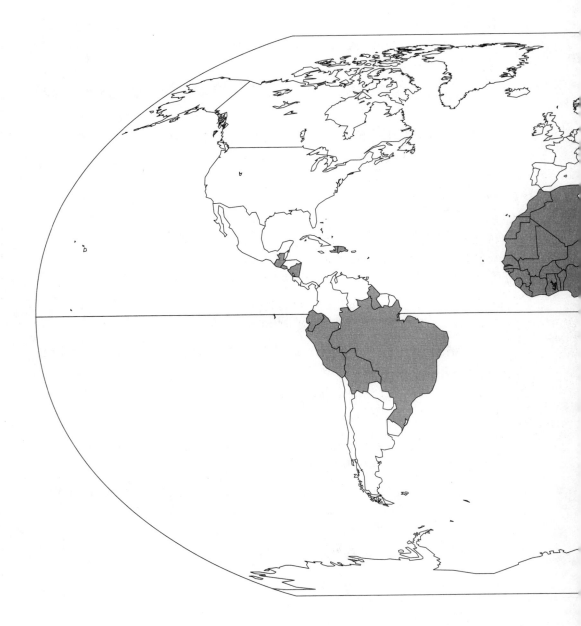

World Summit for Children

One of the most important things that has ever happened to help hungry children took place in September 1990. Seventy-one of the world's leaders (including President Bush) and representatives from 85 more countries—156 altogether—gathered at the United Nations in New York City for the sole purpose of talking about how the world's children are doing.

Their meeting was called the World Summit for Children. During the meeting they came up with something called the World Declaration on the Survival, Development, and Protection of Children. In this document they promised to do something about the children who are dying and suffering from hunger. They put together a 10-part plan in areas such as chronic hunger, lowering infant mortality rates, teaching people to read, and protecting children in time of war. They promised to care for all children—in countries with the most hunger and the least—and to end hunger by the end of this century.

This is the first time that world leaders ever agreed to do something about the problem, all together.

It was a great day for the children of the world! At last, the governments decided to take action. For the first time ever, the presidents and heads of countries promised to save the lives of children. Let's support them!

One of the most important actions any of us can take in ending hunger is to show our leaders that we support their work to end hunger in our own country and around the world.

Tell everybody about the World Summit and the promise the governments made. Tell the world leaders that you are happy they took part in the World Summit for Children—and that you want to make sure they keep their promise.

Another important document that many of the leaders who came to the World Summit signed is called the United Nations Convention on the Rights of the Child. It is about the rights of children, all children.

As soon as the leader of a country signs the Convention, it becomes a law in that country. Almost every country on earth has now ratified (signed) the Convention. But not all.

This is what the Convention says about the basic rights of children around the world:

Every child has

★ *The right to affection, love, and understanding*

★ *The right to adequate nutrition and medical care*

★ *The right to free education*

★ *The right to full opportunity for play and recreation*

★ *The right to a name and nationality*

★ *The right to special care, if handicapped*

★ *The right to be among the first to receive relief in times of disaster*

★ *The right to be a useful member of society and to develop individual abilities*

★ *The right to be brought up in a spirit of peace and universal brotherhood*

★ *The right to enjoy these rights, regardless of race, color, sex, religion, nationality, or social origin*

If the countries really honor the Convention, and take action on the Declaration, we will actually see the day when children are no longer dying of hunger.

Agreeing that these should be the rights of children is the first step.

Making them happen in every country in the world is another matter. That will take lots of work, money, and resources.

That's where kids like you come in.

Find out whether your country has agreed to these rights for children by ratifying (passing) the Convention. Ask your mom or dad. If they don't know, ask your teacher or principal. If they don't know, head for the library. If you find that your country has not ratified the Convention, get to work! Write letters! Call! Let your government officials know that you want them to guarantee these rights for children where you live. Invite others to do the same.

If your country has ratified the Convention, tell people the good news. Ask them to support the laws and spending that will make these rights come true.

What is it like to be hungry?

Africa is where many of the hungry people in the world live. A story about a family who lives in the western part of Africa begins on page 34.

As you read it, see what you can find out about the lives of kids in that part of Africa.

Also, see whether you would say they are suffering from hunger.

A Day Like Any Other Day

Nine-year-old Osman got out of bed. His bed was a thin mat on the dirt floor that he shared with three of his brothers. His mother's and sisters' mats nearby were already empty. He went outside, blinking his eyes in the light of the rising sun. He dipped himself a bit of water out of a jug by the door, and walked over to the hole his family used for a toilet.

◆ Coming back to the house, he saw his mother and sisters returning from the river with the water jugs on their heads. Even his little sister Amina was helping. He smiled at her, letting her know he was proud of her and thought she was doing a good job. Although she was only four years old, she had a big bundle of sticks on her head. Ever since she discovered how to carry a bundle of firewood on her head, she collected as many sticks as she could carry. Then she balanced them on her head for the whole mile-long walk home. It wasn't a lot of wood, but every little bit helped. She was very proud of herself to be helping out. ◆ Osman went back inside the

34

house and woke his brothers up. In a few minutes
they left on their three-mile walk to school in a
neighboring village. On the way to school they met other

AFRICA

children from their village. The whole group raced most of
the way there. Even though he was small for his age, Osman
almost always won, as he was a very fast runner. ◆ When
they got to school, the teacher was passing out breakfast.
Every morning the children were given little biscuits or bowls
of rice, and sometimes they drank milk made from powder.

Osman was glad to eat the food at
school. It was often better than the food at home. He especially
liked it when the biscuits had little bits of raisins in them. ◆
The teacher told them that the money for the food and for
school supplies had been donated by schoolchildren in North

35

America. She described the schools in America, and the children could hardly believe it. ◆ Imagine—every child in America got a desk, there were rooms full of books, and they even had television. Osman and his friends had never seen a television. The idea of a movie in a box seemed like magic to them. ◆ While the other brothers went off to school, seven-year-old Abdullai and his mother and sisters went about their workday. Even though Abdullai was old enough to go to school, he stayed home and watched the family goats instead. When he was three years old, he got very sick with polio, and it left him with a painful limp that made it hard for him to walk. Three miles to school was simply too far for him to go. ◆ Every morning his sisters Radia and Ekila, who were 11 and 10, fed the babies a little cold rice left over from dinner. Then, leaving Amina to watch over the babies, they went out to the field to help their mother, who was already at work. The three of them weeded for hours, before the sun got too hot, and then went home to make the morning meal. Radia helped her mother build a small fire while Ekila cut up some vegetables.

◆ When it was ready, they hungrily sat down on the ground in front of the house to eat. The girls never even thought to ask their mother what they would have, since they ate the same thing every day: a small scoop of rice with a spicy red sauce and some green vegetables. But at least they had food to eat. Radia was old enough to remember the year all the vegetables in the garden had died, and there hadn't been anything to eat for many days. ◆ When they finished eating, they went to work in the fields again, taking Amina and the babies with them this time. Mother carried the littlest one on her back. They worked for a long time in the hot sun. Finally it was time to prepare dinner. It was a long day, and a lot of work. But Radia, Ekila, and Amina didn't mind working so much. All the girls in the village worked, and the boys played and went to school. That's just how it was. ◆ After school, the boys returned home. ◆ "Mother," Osman asked, "do you think that Father will come home soon? One of the boys at school said his father just came home, and he brought them sweets from the city." ◆ "I don't know," his mother replied. "But maybe it will be soon. I hope so." ◆ Like many others in their village, the children knew that their father was in the city to earn money, but they missed him a lot. The family needed the money he earned in the city to buy seeds and other things. Every year he came home in time to plant peanuts and other crops and left until it was time to pick them. Then he went away until it was time to plant again. So for most of the year the family got along without him. ◆ In the evening everyone did the chores, cleaning up around the house, collecting more firewood, going for water and preparing dinner, taking care of the babies, and then everyone sat down in a circle on the ground to eat and talk about the day. Dinner was much like breakfast, a small serving of rice, sauce, and vegetables, with a piece of fruit as a treat. Amina walked over to the pot, hoping to find some extra rice in the bottom, but it was empty. ◆ By the time they finished dinner it was getting dark. Sometimes they stayed up late by the light of a kerosene lamp, but not always, since they couldn't always afford to buy kerosene. Tonight they were out of kerosene, and so they went to bed. ◆◆

What do you think? Is Osman's family suffering from hunger?

Do you think it is serious?

The answer to both is: yes.

They are suffering from a **kind** of hunger, and it **is** serious.

You see, there are two kinds of hunger, not just one.

The kind of hunger that Osman's family is suffering from is called **chronic hunger**. Chronic means something that doesn't go away—it just goes on and on and on.

Most people don't know about chronic hunger.

Most people know about the other kind of hunger, the one called **famine**.

It is important to know the difference between the two because they are caused by very different things. And they are solved in very different ways.

Famine = Emergency

A famine is an emergency. It's when children and grownups suddenly have just about no food at all.

Famines often happen when there has been no rain and all the crops die, or when many, many families are forced to leave their homes because of war or another disaster and they cannot grow or buy food any longer.

People starve to death when there is a famine.

What people in a famine need right away is—food.

What You Can Do

When you hear on TV or in school that a famine is taking place somewhere in the world, ask your family and your friends and your friends' families to please help. Ask them to send money right away.

Some of the groups that work to save lives when there is a famine are listed starting on page 158.

Famines are serious when they happen.

But, amazingly, **many more children suffer and die from chronic hunger than from famine**.

Chronic Hunger—How It Works

If you were to visit a country where there are many hungry people, perhaps you would see a child walking along the road with her mother.

"What a cute little girl," you might say, thinking she was about four.

The problem is that the child is not really four at all. She is seven and a half and her body has not grown properly.

Why?

Well, at home she probably gets food—rice and beans or some sweet potatoes or vegetables—but she and her brothers and sisters and family never get *enough* to eat. They are always a bit hungry.

Children suffering from chronic hunger do not starve to death the way children in a famine do. But their bodies and minds never really get enough healthy food to grow properly.

And so they don't.

They are small, very small for their ages.

Then, because their bodies are not strong enough to fight off the diseases, when they get sick they often die.

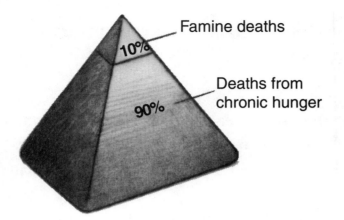

Famine deaths

10%

Deaths from chronic hunger

90%

Ninety percent of all hunger deaths are caused by chronic hunger. The other 10 percent are caused by famines.

WHAT??! HUNH?? IMPOSSIBLE!!

What You Can Do

Ask people in your family how many kinds of hunger they know about. Unless you have a pretty unusual family, they probably know only about famine, not chronic hunger.

If we plan to end hunger, we really need to understand about chronic hunger—since it's the kind of hunger that is causing most of the suffering.

As we saw, Osman's family had food. Maybe not a lot of it, but they were not starving to death. People suffering from chronic hunger do not starve to death.

But the children with chronic hunger are usually small for their age, and weak.

So, when they get sick—say they get a cold or the measles, as we all do—instead of getting better, their weak bodies simply cannot fight the disease. And so they die—of a cold, or from diarrhea, or from things that healthy children would never die of.

Someone could say, "Hey, they died from the measles or from diarrhea, not from hunger!" But it was hunger, not enough food month after month, year after year, that weakened them so badly that something as simple as measles or a cold could kill them.

47

When there is a famine, it means people are starving and we know we need to send food—right away.

But with chronic hunger the people already have some food. People suffering from chronic hunger need something— something more than just food.

About the Solutions— Can We End It?

What's the answer?

The solution is for hungry people to have a chance to improve their own lives—so that they can grow more food themselves or earn more money to buy their food. Otherwise, they will continue to need someone to give them food, forever.

Many hungry people do not have the very basic things that we might think you just can't live without. If we didn't have these basics, we would most likely find ourselves sick and hungry as well.

What do the hungry people need?

- An education, so that they can learn to read—especially the women—and learn about better ways to grow food, or do their jobs, or take care of their families, or find out what is happening in the rest of the world.

- Loans, so they can start a small business, or buy some land, or seeds, or tools to grow enough food to feed their families or earn enough money to buy the things their families need.

- Materials to build roads, so they can take their food to market, and wells, so they can have clean water, and schools, so that their children can learn how to make their lives better.

- Health workers, to teach mothers how to keep their children from dying when they get sick, and how to have only the number of babies they want; health clinics, where children can get shots to keep them from catching some of the diseases in the first place.

This is what we mean by giving the hungry people a break, a chance to improve their own lives.

Kids can tell adults who want to help end hunger about the importance of giving hungry people not just food, but the chance to have a good life so that they can feed themselves. Otherwise, people who want to help just keep sending food!

Reading + Girls = Ending Hunger

What on earth does reading have to do with ending hunger? you might wonder. Well, think about it—what if your mother couldn't read?

- She wouldn't know what shots you should get.

- She couldn't read the label on medicines.

- She couldn't get a good-paying job.

- She couldn't read articles on how to prepare food and she couldn't learn one single thing in the library.

- She couldn't read the paper to know what is happening in the world.

- She couldn't read about meetings coming up that could help her.

- She couldn't help you do well with your studies so you could get ahead.

- People would not pay much attention to her or take her very seriously.

Studies have found that babies whose mothers were taught to read had a 40 percent better chance of staying alive than those whose mothers did not know how to read. That's a big difference!

Some people even say that teaching mothers to read is the **most** important step that can be taken to end hunger!

In the story on the next page, which takes place in India, the children are worried about their families. They take action to help give their families a chance to improve their lives so they won't go hungry.

The Children Get Help

INDIA

The day began like any other. Ram awoke to see his older brother standing in the dark saying it was time to get up and get ready for the day. He sat up in his little bed, letting his feet hang down over the edge and touch the cleanly swept dirt floor. Looking around, he saw his younger brothers, Kazi and Bimal, rubbing their eyes and stretching. They slept together in one bed, and when they stretched they kicked each other. His sisters, Sita and Asha, had already gotten up to make the fire. The baby was still asleep. ◆ Ram got up quickly and went out to the front room. Father was already there, with a cup of tea in one hand, eating chapati, the flat round bread that the girls were baking in the fire. Ram sat down on the grass mat next to him, followed by his brothers. The girls were busy making more chapatis, cleaning up, doing other girl chores. After the boys and their father finished their breakfast, the girls and their mother sat down to eat. ◆ Ram went out and picked some bananas and mangoes from the trees in their yard. Putting the fruit in a sack over his shoulder, he climbed onto the family bicycle and rode along the dirt road to market. Just as he started off, Mother came running out of the house, yelling that he should buy some oil.

◆ "Okay!" Ram yelled back. ◆ "And some chili," she added.

◆ "Yes, Mother." He was hoping she would ask him to buy a handful of nuts for tonight's supper also, but she didn't. Oh well, you can't expect to have treats every day. Though he was only nine years old, Ram did the buying and selling for the family. Every morning before school he brought something to the market to sell. Sometimes he sold mangoes and bananas, sometimes onions—whatever he could find in the garden. He would settle into his favorite spot on a corner in front of the main market and spread out his goods. Then he would sit there until everything was sold. If he finished in time, he could go to school. ◆ This day he had been able to sell everything. Grabbing his pencil and notebook, he raced down the dirt path to the school. It was a small two-room building with lots of windows to let in the light. Everyone sat on the floor. Ram got there just as the teacher was calling everyone inside. Then the math lesson began. Ram was good at math and was able to

copy the problems from the board quickly. Waiting for others to finish, he turned and looked out the window. He saw his sister Sita walk by carrying a jug on her head, on the way to the well for water. She was with a group of women who were carrying clothing to the well to do their washing. ◆ Suddenly everyone heard a funny sound coming from outside. They all looked out the window. One of the boys sitting near the window stuck his head way out to see better. ◆ "A car!" he cried excitedly. ◆ The teacher let the children go outside to see. It was a car, with strangers inside. The teacher went to greet them and brought them inside. The children hurried back to their places so that they could find out what was happening. ◆ One of the women said that they had come from the city to help the villagers stay healthy, and that they were going to set up a clinic and give shots which would help keep the children from getting sick. She called the shots "immunizations." The visitors took out some puppets and did a little show about how kids could die without the shots. ◆ Ram already knew they could die from getting sick; he didn't need the show. His baby brother had died four years before, when Ram was only five, but he remembered how sad it was. His brother wasn't even one year old when he died. ◆ "Please, children, go home and tell your parents about these shots. Please ask them to bring you and all the children of this village to the clinic to be immunized," the lady said. ◆ At home, Ram's parents agreed to send the children to the clinic, though Ram thought he noticed some sadness come into his mother's eyes when they talked about babies that could be saved by immunizations. ◆ One evening later that week, everything was ready for dinner, but Father wasn't home yet. It was unusual for him to be so late, and Mother began to worry. Just as she was about to send Ram out to look for him, they saw him coming. They could tell by how he was walking that something was wrong. Bimal and Sita ran to meet him.

◆ "What is it, Father?" they asked. "Why do you look so unhappy?" ◆ Stopping to look at them both, he shook his head. "Wait until after dinner, and then I will tell you and your mother. You are old enough now. You should begin to learn about these things." ◆ And so they ate dinner in silence, everyone too worried about what was the matter to talk about anything else. Finally dinner was finished. They lit the kerosene lamp. Now it was time to talk. ◆ "The moneylender came by today," Father said. "We are behind in our payments, and he says we must pay him by the end of the month, or he will not lend us more money for the next year. But we don't have enough money to pay him, or even to buy seeds for the next planting. I spoke with my brothers and friends, and they have the same problem. We all agree he charges us too much, but what can we do?" ◆ "Why do we owe him money? Why do we need the money from him, Father?" Ram asked. ◆ "That is a long story. You see, many years ago I borrowed money to buy the plow we now use. You know the plow?" The children nodded. ◆ "Well, I was supposed to pay back the amount the moneylender had let me borrow, plus some extra money. That is called interest. But I couldn't pay him back that year because we didn't have much rain that year, and we didn't grown enough wheat. I didn't have any extra money. So the next year we owed him even more money. The same thing keeps happening every year. We never have enough extra money to pay him back." ◆ "What can we do?" Sita asked.

◆ "We owe him the money, and that is all there is to it," her father answered. "Perhaps we should sell some of our animals." ◆ "We can't do that," Mother said. "We need the milk from the goats, the eggs from the chickens, and the water buffalo pulls the plow. We'll have to find another way."

◆ Everyone went to bed worried that night. What would they do? ◆ Ram talked to his friends about it the next day at school. They, too, had the same problem at their homes. The children decided to tell their teacher about it. Ram was chosen as the one to explain the problem. ◆ "Teacher," he said, "we are all from poor families, and there is a man who says if we don't give him money, he won't help us buy seeds. Without his help, Father says, we won't be able to plant our wheat and other crops this year, and we will be hungry. Can you help us?" ◆ Their teacher looked at them thoughtfully. "Maybe I can," she replied. "You know, I just read a story in the newspaper about a government program that lends money to farmers. Maybe they would help your families. I will write a letter to the government office and we will find out." ◆ And so, because the children asked her, the teacher wrote a letter to the section of the government that is supposed to help farmers. ◆ It was three weeks before they got a reply. The children had almost given up hope. The letter said that a government worker would come and visit their village the following week. The letter also said that organizations from some other countries might be able to help out as well. ◆ "How will it work?" the children asked the teacher when she had finished reading them the letter. ◆ "Well, the government is going to lend people in this village some money, and all the farmers are also going to put in some money. Then they will take turns borrowing the whole batch of money to buy what they need. When they pay it back, someone else can borrow it next. That way everyone will get a turn, and they don't need to pay any interest to the moneylender," the teacher explained. ◆ The children began to talk excitedly about what their families would do with the money. ◆ "My father will use it to buy better seeds, the ones that produce strong and healthy wheat. Then we will be able to grow more wheat, and pay back the moneylender and still have plenty to sell!" Ram told everyone. ◆ Ram went home that night and told his family the good news. At first they didn't believe him. Sita told him to stop making up stories. His mother said that she knew he was worried, they all were, but somehow they would make it work. "But this is how it will work!" Ram told them. "You'll see." ◆ The next week they did see. The extension agent from the government organized the farmers to put their money together to buy seeds and tools at a lower price, and to set up a revolving loan fund. ◆ Meanwhile, a representative from another organization announced that they were going to give several calves to the children of the village, since they had been the ones to call for help. The calves would be raised by all the children together, with the help of their teacher and parents. The milk from the calves when they grew to be cows would be given to the children of the village. Any extra milk would be sold to pay for school supplies. ◆ "Where did the calves come from?" Ram asked. The person from the Heifer Project explained that a group of schoolchildren in America had raised the money to buy the calves. ◆ "There is only one other thing," the lady from the Heifer Project told them. "The first calf born to each of these when they get older must be given back to us, so we can give them to another village that needs them." ◆ All the children happily agreed, glad to know that they would be able to help another group of children in the same way they'd been helped. ◆◆

Did you recognize the chances the villagers—including the children—were given to improve their lives in the last story?

The Child Survival Campaign

One thing that is saving the lives of hungry children is called the Child Survival Campaign. The visitors to Ram's school were part of it.

People working with child survival have figured out a way to save millions and millions of kids' lives each year. They have found **easy, inexpensive** ways to keep many of those hungry kids from getting sick in the first place, and to keep lots of the ones who are sick from dying.

This is an example of giving people a chance to improve their lives.

You can find out about the Child Survival Campaign and how you can support it on pages 93–98 and in the "50 Things Kids Can Do" section.

Neat. Maybe we should get a cow, too!

Remember the African boy Osman and his family? This next story tells what happened to them when there was a famine.

It also shows how they were given a chance to improve their lives in some very important ways through the Child Survival Campaign.

When Things Got Worse

AFRICA

It was a hot, dry day. It had been that way for almost as long as Osman could remember. They were in the midst of one of the worst droughts in years. He and his brothers had stopped going to school long ago, because they didn't have the energy to walk the three miles each way. They missed the morning meal they got at school. They hadn't harvested any rice this year, or anything else, for that matter. Everything had died because it was so dry. And then the food they had saved from the year before ran out, too. Now all they had to eat was a sort of stew made from roots and weeds they picked, but even these were getting hard to find. And the stew was not very filling.

◆ Osman looked up and saw his brother, Abdullai, watching three goats. All the rest of the family's goats had died from lack of food and water. The three that were left looked skinny and sad. Abdullai looked sad, too. Osman went to talk to him. ◆ "Hello, little brother," he said. "Cheer up. Maybe Father will come home today and bring us something from the city. Mother said he will come soon. Don't give up." ◆ "I haven't given up. But I miss my other goats. They were my friends. And these goats no longer play with me—they don't do anything but eat the dry grass. I just sit here all day feeling sad and hungry." ◆ Lately when their mother and the others headed off to get water, Abdullai was asked to watch not only the babies, but his four-year-old sister Amina, too. She had not been well lately, and could no longer walk the mile to get water. Then the water hole near the house had dried up, and even this one, which they spent four hours going to and from each day, had just a little water left in it. Their mother was worried that they would all get sick from the muddy water, but they had no choice. They needed water and that was all they could get.

◆ So from then on Abdullai had three little ones to watch. They would sit together in a group near the goats, the little ones asleep or lying without moving or talking very much. They did not have the energy to play and so they were easy to look after. ◆ When the rest of the family returned from getting water, they would all help look for things to put in the stew, and also for sticks to make a fire to cook it with. Ten-year-old Ekila carried the baby on her back as she worked. When they put the roots and plants in a pot of water on the fire and ate the stew, it was the only meal they had each day. ◆ After they ate, they would do what chores they had the energy for, sweeping around the house and cleaning up after the meal, and then they would just sit. Even the boys were too weak to play. Mostly they just sat and stared or talked quietly. ◆ Then one day, as they were sitting in the dirt in the front yard, their father came home. They had almost given up hoping for him. It was the first happy day in a long, long time.

He brought some food with him, a sack

of rice and some wheat that he had gotten from one of the organizations that helps families when there is a famine or some other kind of emergency. For the first time in weeks, they had a proper meal. Maybe now things would be better. ◆

Soon after their father came home, Amina got sick. She had been very weak for a long time, but this was much worse. No matter what they offered her, she would not eat. Whenever they did get her to eat something, she threw it up. She ran a very high fever, and had constant diarrhea. She was very quickly getting thinner and thinner, and could barely lift her head from the pillow. Mother and Father talked softly together, trying not to frighten the children. Everyone loved Amina; she was the favorite of the whole family. Everyone tried hard to help her get well. ◆ "She can have my dinner, really she can," Abdullai offered, forgetting his own hungry stomach.

◆ Finally they decided that Father should take her to the health clinic. It would take him two days to walk to the clinic in another town, carrying Amina the whole way. There had not been money to build a clinic in their village or to pay for a health worker to visit. ◆ The whole family gathered around as Father wrapped her in a cloth and put her over his shoulder. She seemed too light in his arms. ◆ "Goodbye, my little flower," Mother said softly. Everyone stood in the road, waving goodbye. ◆ It was more than a week before their father returned—without Amina. ◆ "She was gone before I got there," Father said softly. "They said she had lost too much weight and too much liquid. There was nothing they could do."

◆ Mother started to cry. "My poor baby, my poor sweet child." She was silent for a moment, and tears wet her eyes. Then she said quietly, "At least she will not hurt any longer."

◆ Some of the others started to cry for Amina as well. They had all loved their little sister. She had been a source of real joy in their lives, with her little songs and her big brown eyes that seemed so full of trust and love. Now she was gone.

◆ "There is one other thing," Father said. "When I got to the clinic, the health worker told me that if this ever happens again, to any of you"—he stopped for a moment to look around at the children—"that we must give you some of this special powder." With that, he took out several shiny little packages of white powder. "We must mix it with boiled water if any of our other children suffer as Amina did." ◆ The children crowded around to see this magical powder that could have saved their baby sister, that could someday save them. "ORS," Osman read softly. "I wonder what it means. I wonder how it works. I wonder..." and with that he silently made a decision. He decided that when he grew up he would do everything he could to bring a clinic to his village. He would study hard so that he could be the village health worker, and find out more about this mysterious ORS. No other babies in their village would need to die, he promised himself. ◆ Father told more about his trip to the clinic. "People all over are having a hard time. Some are even worse off than we are. But some are doing better. Some of the nearby villages got money and supplies from organizations with funny names like UNICEF and Oxfam and CARE. Nearby they have put in a well with money given by Save the Children. They now have water for their goats and can water their crops." ◆ A well in their own village. The very thought was almost more than Radia could imagine. Think of the hundreds and hundreds of hours that she and her mother would save if they did not have to go so far for water! ◆ Father continued. "Some of the villages receive bags of rice and wheat from organizations from far away.  In some of the villages, they will give you rice, even if you are not from the village. I found one, a day's walk from here, where we can go for food every two weeks if we need it. Osman and I will leave for there tomorrow." ◆ And so they made it through the drought and famine that year, with the help from people they had never met. It wasn't easy even so. All but one of the goats died, and everyone got sick, and sometimes they didn't think they could go on, but they did. ◆ Finally the rains came, and they got seeds from the same place where they were getting the rice, and they planted them. Before long they had vegetables to eat along with their rice. At first it was hard to work in the fields, for they didn't have the energy to work the way they used to. But they knew they had to grow food and so they worked anyway. Even the boys helped. They didn't go back to school for a long time so that they could help. ◆ One very good thing happened. Father and some of the men talked with the people from the organizations about getting a well in their village. They also talked about building a storage place for their grain. The villagers agreed to put some of the rice they grew each year into the grain storage house. Then if there was another drought, they would have both water from their well and food that had been saved. Never again would they be that hungry. Never again. ◆ Little Abdullai dreamed about a clinic for the village, a place to take sick children. "Save the Children," he said softly to himself, remembering the name of one of the groups his father had mentioned that were helping his village. Thinking of his little sister Amina, and then looking at the other babies, "Save the Children," he repeated. "What a good idea." ◆◆

Let's change the subject for a moment and talk about pennies.

Yes, pennies.

Did you know that **four pennies** can buy something unbelievably important: a child's eyesight?

No way. Now I know they're lying. Four cents can't buy *anything*.

I don't even pick up pennies when I see them on the street.

I *like* pennies. I have a whole collection of them.

Each year, 350,000 children go blind because they don't get enough Vitamin A in their food.

Is Vitamin A hard to find? No.

It is in green vegetables and in yellow and orange ones.

Or, if there are no vegetables around, children can be given two Vitamin A pills each year, and then they will not go blind.

The cost of each Vitamin A pill? Two cents.

Four pennies a year to keep a child from going blind.

Organize an "I Can See" penny collection week at your school.

Let all the classes know that you (and some of your friends) are going to be coming around on a certain day with a *big* jar. In the jar you want all the pennies everyone can bring in. (A group of elementary school students in Florida collected 53,000 pennies in three days!)

You can make some posters in advance, letting everyone know why you're going to be collecting the pennies—letting them know what their four cents will buy.

Be sure to let the kindergartners in on the project. They will be thrilled to know that there is something they can do to help hungry children.

You can send the money to the International Eye Foundation (see page 162) or Helen Keller International (page 161).

From now on, you and your friends will know what to do with all the pennies you find!

In this next story, one of the Indian children almost goes blind, because he isn't getting Vitamin A.

Vitamin A Saves the Day

"Hey, Bimal, are you sleeping?" one of the cousins yelled when Bimal didn't even try to catch the ball they threw to him.

INDIA

◆ "Leave him alone. He doesn't want to play," his brother, Ram, told them. "Can't you see he's just sitting there?" ◆ The boys went back to playing as the light continued to get dimmer. It was a warm evening, and they had come out after dinner to play until dark. Bimal had been playing, but then he drifted away from the game to sit by himself on the side. ◆ The next night the same thing happened. Again Bimal went off by himself in the middle of the game. This time Ram got worried. ◆ "What's wrong? Why don't you want to play with us?" he asked. ◆ "It's not that," Bimal replied. "It's too hard to catch the ball. I don't like to play." ◆ Ram didn't understand. At the beginning of every game Bimal was always excited, and eager to play. But midway through, he always stopped. Ram decided to talk to his parents about it. ◆ The next morning before breakfast, he told his father about Bimal's strange behavior. ◆ "I don't understand, Father," he said. "Bimal starts to play with us, right after dinner, but as we continue to play the game he always stops and sits off by himself. If we throw him the ball, he acts as if he doesn't even see it." ◆ "Bimal," his father asked, "why don't you play?" ◆ "It's too hard to catch the ball in the dark," was Bimal's answer. ◆ "But it isn't dark yet when we play," Ram pointed out. "We come home before dark." ◆ Their mother and father looked at each other with worry. They had heard stories of children who start off not being able to see at night, and soon they cannot see during the day either. They didn't want that to happen to Bimal. They decided to take him to the doctor. ◆ There was no doctor anywhere nearby, so they arranged to take a bus trip to the clinic in the big town. Grandmother, who lived with them, agreed to watch over the other children while they were gone. ◆ It took a long time to get there. The road to their village was too narrow and bumpy for a bus or car to pass over, so they had to walk for the first part of the trip. They knew the way since their first baby, who would have been two years older than Bimal, had gotten very sick and had died in that clinic. They hoped they would have better luck on this trip. ◆ Bimal wasn't scared. He had never traveled on a bus before and thought it was great fun. He laughed when a lady got on with three wildly clucking chickens which she tried to have sit still on her lap. ◆ At the clinic, the doctor let them know that Bimal had a disease, and that if it were not treated it would lead to blindness. It had a long name: *xerophthalmia.* The doctor said that they were lucky

they had caught it so early. If Ram had not noticed it and told them about it, Bimal would almost certainly have gone blind. As it was, the doctor told them that what they needed to do was to make sure he ate more vegetables, so that he got enough Vitamin A. Then he gave Bimal a Vitamin A tablet, and sent him outside while he continued to talk to his parents.

◆ "This is serious, but luckily it's easy to fix. If he and your other children eat their green and yellow vegetables, they will be fine. When there are no vegetables in your garden, give them these vitamin tablets." ◆ Bimal and his mother and father thanked the doctor and walked out into the bright sunshine. Bimal didn't say anything. He just looked at everything, all the way home, smiling from ear to ear. ◆◆

Ending hunger is going to cost money. Many experts say it would cost the world about $20 billion a year to end hunger.

Is $20 billion a lot of money?

Sure, if we compare it to how much money one person has or one family has. But compared to how much money a whole country, or the whole world, has to spend, it actually isn't that much.

Millions of children are weak and sick with hunger—but it's not because there is not enough money.

We have the money.

We just spend it on other things.

Think about it for a moment—what is money for, anyway?

How Much Is $20 Billion?

- It is the amount of money people spend on cigarettes—every 60 days.

- It is the cost of 40 bomber planes or 5 aircraft carriers.

- It is the amount of money that people in the United States of America spend on toys and sports equipment each year.

- It is the amount of money people in the U.S. spend on going to the beauty parlor and barber every year.

- It is what the world spends **every eight days** on military expenses.

- It is the amount of money needed to save 40,000 children a day from dying.

People spend money on things that are important to them.

If ending hunger were important enough to the world, if the lives of millions of children a year were important enough to us as a human family, we would want to spend our money on saving those lives. We would want to spend the money to end the suffering.

Right?

What would happen if everyone *really* wanted to end hunger!?!

You can see that one of the jobs kids can do is to make people everywhere realize how many kids are suffering from hunger, and to let them know that we need to spend our time and our money to end hunger.

Many of us who can afford to, give our own money to the organizations working to end hunger.

Kids and adults can give their own money, and they can give money that they raise from friends and other people.

How does the money we give help end hunger?

We usually give it to people and organizations in our own country who work with the hungry people all around the world. There are **thousands** of organizations working to care for the hungry. Many of them are run by the hungry people themselves. Some of them you may already know about, like CARE and UNICEF.

You can find the names and addresses of some of the many organizations working on ending hunger starting on page 158.

How Do They Help?

Some of the organizations working on ending hunger give out food or medicine or supplies during famines and other emergencies. What they do is called "relief" or "aid." Of course, sometimes it is hard for them to deliver the food and supplies that people send, if there are no roads, or no trucks to carry the shipments to where the hungry people are.

Other organizations working on ending hunger spend the money helping the hungry people improve their lives so that they can raise food to feed their families or earn enough money to buy it. This work is called "development." Often these organizations work with the people who are suffering from chronic hunger.

These organizations use our donations to do things such as buy seeds and tools, or to teach parents and health workers how to keep children healthy, or to teach people how to read, or to supply goats or cows or wells, or to build roads or schools, or to teach people how to take good care of the soil and how to plant trees so the forests will grow back.

Other organizations let people know the facts about hunger and ending it. Through videos, newspapers, pamphlets, letters, and conferences, they give people all over the world an opportunity to get involved. They often suggest writing to lawmakers to ask them to change the laws so that enough money gets spent on ending hunger.

Then there are the organizations working on population, the environment, peace, health, and family planning. They are helping to eliminate the situations that cause hunger.

Each of these plays an important part in ending hunger.

What about hunger in countries like the United States of America? Is there any? The answer is yes. In fact, about one out of every five children goes to bed hungry every night in the United States.

Most of the hungry people in the U.S. don't have enough money to buy the food they need for themselves and their families. They need more than just food—they need opportunities to get better jobs.

There are organizations and groups in the U.S. helping the hungry and homeless by giving them food, by finding jobs for them, and by helping them get a better education.

As you get involved in ending hunger, you can support ending hunger in your country as well as in countries where there is a lot of hunger. When you raise money, you may want to give some of the money to the organizations working to end hunger in your own area. In the United States call the United Way (their telephone number is in the white pages of your phone book) to find out who is working on ending hunger in your area. Or talk with your neighborhood librarian. He or she probably has a whole file on the subject.

The story on the next page is about some children living in the United States who are hungry. Who knows? They could even live near you.

A Place for Us

Shana woke up first. She sat up and looked around, still half-asleep. The bed she was sitting on was actually a pad on the floor. On the other end of the same bed her little brother, Jerome, was still sleeping. Her mother was next to them, asleep on a cot. As Shana looked around, she saw what had woken her. People all around them were folding up their cots and tossing their blankets into a big laundry bin. The cots clanged as they were stacked against the wall. ◆ Shana woke up her mother and brother and they all got dressed quickly, packing up their two bags of belongings, and then put their bedding away like everyone else. They weren't allowed to leave anything in the homeless shelter during the day. While they were standing in line for their breakfast, a dry roll and some milk or coffee, one of the women who ran the shelter approached Shana's mother with the news. They would have to move on. She was very sorry, the lady said, but that's just how it was. ◆ Shana didn't understand why. For some reason, homeless shelters had rules about how long you could stay in them. Even though they had no place to go to, Shana, Jerome, and their mother had already been kicked out of four other shelters, and now it was happening again. ◆ The lady suggested they try two other shelters. One was a mile away, and the other was way across town. Shana's mother decided to try the closer one first. Shana couldn't go to school that morning, since she wouldn't have known where to find her mother and brother when she got out. So the three of them picked up their two bags and headed out. ◆ Jerome was particularly sad about the move.

He liked that shelter better than any of the other ones they'd stayed at. Some of the men there had been really nice to him. They let him sit with them at dinner and told him stories and sometimes even gave him things. Not fancy things, of course, but for a kid who has nothing, almost anything can be a gift. He still had the little ends of colored wire that one of them had given him. They were great for making little people and animal shapes, and he played with them a lot. Jerome would miss those guys. He walked along with his head down, dragging his feet. ◆ "Come on, don't worry," Shana said to him. "There will probably be other nice men at the next shelter." But Jerome was remembering the first shelter they stayed at, where people yelled at the kids for making too much noise, no matter how quiet they were. He and Shana were afraid someone would hit them, and tried so hard to be quiet. What if the new shelter was like that one? ◆ It took them almost an hour to get to the shelter. It was raining hard that day, and they didn't own an umbrella. By the time they got there they were all wet. When they knocked on the office door, no one answered. The door was locked. Shana found another door that was open, and they walked in and found the janitor, who told them that the shelter didn't open until dinnertime, and to come back. But what would they do until then? Where could they wait without getting wet all day? ◆ "Mama, could we go to the other shelter?" Jerome asked. "The lady said it was smaller. I don't like this one; it's too big and scary." ◆ "It's a long trip," their mother answered, "and we might not even get in once we're there. I don't have any money for lunch. Are you sure you want to go?" ◆ "Uh-huh!" they both said at the same time. Shana wanted to get away as far as possible from the school she had been going to. She was sure that anywhere else would be better. The only thing she really liked about that school was that you got free lunches. A lot of the kids didn't like the food at school and hardly ate any of it, but Shana thought it was delicious. She used to eat all of her lunch and then sneak whatever extra she could find into her pockets—whatever wasn't too messy. Her mother and Jerome usually didn't get any lunch. ◆ At school she was always being sent to the principal's office for falling asleep in class. A few times she was sent to the office for stealing. The only thing she ever took was candy. She knew she shouldn't, but it looked so good, and that was the only way she'd ever get any. The other kids could always get more. Besides, they weren't very nice to her. They were always making fun of her and her hand-me-down clothes and shoes, and they never let her play with them. Shana was glad she wouldn't have to go back to that school anymore. Maybe the one near the new shelter would be different. ◆ It took several buses and a lot of walking and waiting in the rain to get there. By the time they arrived they were tired, wet, and hungry. Jerome had started sneezing halfway through the afternoon and his throat hurt. ◆ When they got to the shelter two women let them in. They immediately took charge of the situation. ◆ "Oh, you must be cold," one said. ◆ "And hungry?" the other asked. "But these children need a hot bath and a change of clothes first. We must have something that will fit them in the closet." With that, she led them off down the hall. ◆ "Don't worry about the children," the first woman said to Mother. "They'll be taken care of. As for you, how about a hot shower? You have about 30 minutes until dinnertime."

◆ "What about the paperwork?" Mother asked. ◆ "Not to worry. We got a call from the shelter where you stayed last night, saying you might be coming. The paperwork can wait until after supper." ◆ Dinner was great. It was practically like a party. The food was good and there was plenty of it. The people were nice, too. ◆ Warm and dry in their new hand-me-downs, Shana and Jerome sat next to their mother and watched the other people in the dining room. There were about 10 kids and their mothers, and a few single men and women.

◆ Partway through dinner, one of the boys came over and asked if Jerome wanted to play with him after dinner. Jerome looked up at his mother. ◆ "I guess that would be all right," she said. Jerome smiled shyly. He hadn't had anyone but Shana to play with for a long time. ◆ After dinner everyone went into the TV room. Some of the adults and children watched TV while others talked or played. During a commercial, Shana asked one of the girls who was her age about the school she went to. ◆ "It's okay. They make us do a lot of work, but the kids are pretty nice. They don't act like we're dumb or anything," the girl told her. Shana was glad to hear it. Maybe this school would be better than the last one.

◆ Jerome enjoyed playing with the other boys. Two of them were also four years old. They had so much fun playing together that the people by the television set had to ask them to pipe down. But the adults didn't get too mad since they liked to see the little boys having such a good time. ◆ In talking to some of the other women, Shana's mother found out about a program that would help her get a part-time job while she went back to school. Like Shana's mother, they had also dropped out of high school and thought they weren't very smart. But they said that the program was pretty interesting and not too hard. Shana's mother decided to give it a try. ◆ The next morning they learned more about the shelter. It had a classroom where the grown-ups could study and a playroom with some toys and a TV. There was a dining room and four sleeping rooms that everyone shared. They found out that it was a special family shelter, run by a church, for families and people who really seemed like they wanted to get a job and earn enough money to get back into an apartment of their own. In fact, if they wanted to be able to stay in this shelter, Shana's mother *had* to go back to school and get a job. They would be allowed to stay until they had enough money to make it on their own again. They felt very lucky. ◆ After lunch they went over to the school to sign Shana up for fourth grade. They dropped in at the child-care center next door. It was a special center with a certain number of spaces for poor children. Luckily, a family had just moved away and so there was room in the class for Jerome. He was very excited, since this would be his first time in a school. Plus they got the same free lunches that the kids at the elementary school did! ◆ Shana was happy. She had new friends, a good place to stay, and a new school. And she was happy because her mother and brother were happy, too. ◆ Things were definitely looking up. Shana sure hoped the good luck would last for a while! ◆◆

There is some really great news about what some of the
organizations listed in this book have been up to. As we told
you on page 63, several of them have gotten together to form
something they call the Child Survival Campaign, and it is
really working.

In fact, the Child Survival Campaign has saved **millions of kids' lives** already! What's more, the way they do it is by using very inexpensive, very simple methods. Millions of kids have been saved, and millions and millions more will be saved—if people keep supporting the work of the Child Survival Campaign!

Here is some information about it for you, and so you can tell others about it.

There are four main parts to the Child Survival Campaign. **"GOBI"** is a made-up word that helps us remember the four ways to help kids—hungry and healthy ones—so that they don't get sick. Each letter stands for one way to save millions of children's lives.

Once you know about Child Survival and GOBI, you will be able to tell others about it and ask them to support this important work.

The G in GOBI stands for *growth measuring*

If parents and health workers keep track of how much weight new babies gain by writing it down on a chart, they can see when a baby isn't gaining enough weight and his or her life is in danger. Babies who don't gain enough weight become weak and are almost certain to get sick and die.

Many parents don't know how important it is to keep track of their babies' growth; many don't know how to do it; many more don't have the scales or charts or aren't able to read them.

Another way to keep track of growth is by measuring the size of a child's upper arm.

How does it work? The size of a child's arm does not change much from birth until he or she is five years old.

Baby fat in the arm is normally replaced by muscle, and the size stays pretty much the same. If the arm band shows that the upper arm is getting smaller, parents or health workers know the child is losing too much weight.

Here is an arm band like the ones used all over the world where the Child Survival Campaign is working.

You can make an arm band and try it out if you like. Trace the arm band on this page, then transfer your tracing onto a stiff piece of paper or plastic. Leave the START section white. Color the DANGER section red. Color the GOOD section green.

Now try it out. If the child measures in the green, he or she is well nourished. Someone who measures in the red is too thin.

How does your arm measure?

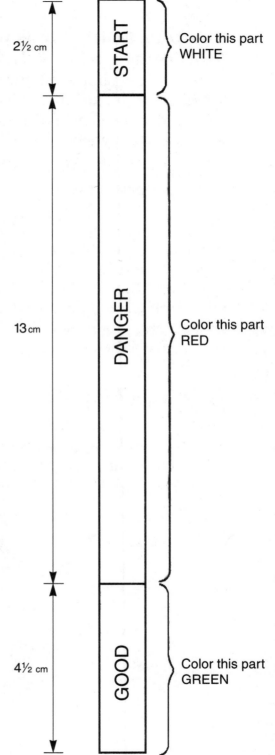

2½ cm

START — Color this part WHITE

13 cm

DANGER — Color this part RED

GOOD — Color this part GREEN

4½ cm

The O in GOBI stands for *ORS*
(oral rehydration salts)

ORS is a very simple mixture of sugar, salt, and clean water. When someone has a very bad case of diarrhea for too long, he or she most likely will die. If the person drinks ORS, he or she almost certainly will live.

Did you know that diarrhea is the greatest killer of children under the age of five?

Actually, it isn't the diarrhea that kills them.

When you have diarrhea, your body loses a lot of liquids. If little babies have diarrhea for a long time, they lose too much liquid and their bodies get too dried out—then they die. When you drink ORS, your body becomes able to absorb or take in much, much more liquid and salt than before. ORS stops the children's bodies from drying out.

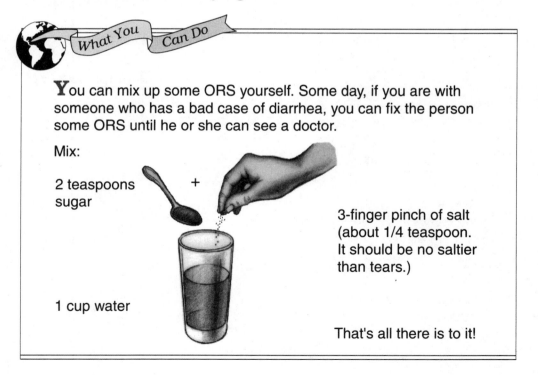

What You Can Do

You can mix up some ORS yourself. Some day, if you are with someone who has a bad case of diarrhea, you can fix the person some ORS until he or she can see a doctor.

Mix:

2 teaspoons sugar

+

3-finger pinch of salt (about 1/4 teaspoon. It should be no saltier than tears.)

1 cup water

That's all there is to it!

This simple mixture can save the lives of the **2.5 million** babies who die from diarrhea each year.

The cost?

Ten cents a packet.

The B in GOBI stands for *breast-feeding*

In some parts of the world women have stopped breast-feeding their babies. They feed them powdered formula instead.

This is dangerous in places where there is a lot of hunger. The water that the mothers mix with the powdered milk is not clean. Babies who drink formula made with the unclean water are twice or three times as likely to die as babies who drink their mother's milk.

Plus formula costs money, and breast milk is free.

Another good thing about breast-feeding is that breast milk helps protect babies from getting many childhood diseases.

Breast-feeding can also help increase the amount of time that goes by before mothers have another baby. That helps to keep families from getting too big to take care of.

So one way to save many children's lives is to let the mothers know how great it would be for their babies if they would breast-feed them.

The I in GOBI stands for *immunizations*

Immunization is another word for a shot, one that you get to keep you from catching a certain sickness.

Do you remember the visitors who came to Ram's school and asked the children to tell their parents to bring all the kids to be immunized? In many countries, children are not allowed in school until they have gotten their shots. (Ask your parents whether you had to prove you had your immunization shots before you could start school.)

In poor countries, most children don't get the shots that would protect them from serious childhood diseases. Since they are suffering from chronic hunger and their bodies are weak, when they catch those diseases they very often die.

Ten dollars is what it costs to immunize a child against measles, polio, whooping cough, tetanus, tuberculosis, and diphtheria.

Thirteen cents is the cost to protect a child against measles. Last year **1.5 million** kids died of measles. A 13-cent shot could have saved their lives.

GOBI: *G*rowth measuring, *O*ral rehydration salts, *B*reast-feeding, and *I*mmunizations—these four things—can save the lives of millions of kids! When you and the kids in your school think of projects to raise money for ending hunger, be sure to keep GOBI in mind.

The next story is about some children who are not hungry, but who decide to get involved in ending hunger. Kids pretty much like you.

Trick-Or-Treating for UNICEF

Ellen rushed home from school,
ran through the kitchen, dropped her books onto
the table, and ran up the stairs two at a time to
see what her mother had bought her. Throwing open
the door to her bedroom, she let out an excited squeal.
"Wow! Mom, you got the one I wanted!" ◆ There on her bed
was the neatest Halloween costume ever. She had seen it last
week in the store. It was *sooooo* great. But her mom had said it
was too expensive. She wanted her to wear the same one as
last year. Yuck! ◆ All week Ellen had done extra things
around the house, and even asked the neighbors to give her
odd jobs. She did everything she could think of to earn money
for the costume. But it wasn't enough. Yesterday, the day
before Halloween, she had only $18.74, and the costume cost
$35. If she had one more week, maybe she could have done it.

◆ When she told her mother about the problem, her mother
took the $18.74 and told her she'd see what she could find at
the store. Ellen had given up on getting the one she really

wanted and just hoped for something that wasn't too dumb. Even though her mom was great, it was a risk. And now, there it was. Her costume! ◆ Her mother came down the hall to her room, smiling. "They were having a special sale since it was the last day, and it was marked down 20 percent. It still cost $28.00, but I decided that we would pay the difference. What are you waiting for? Try it on!" ◆ Ellen was so excited that she had a hard time getting into the costume. Her mother had to untangle her. Once dressed, she ran next door to her friend Sebastian's house to show him. ◆ "Amazing!" Sebastian said when he opened the door. "That is fantastic. I can't wait to go trick-or-treating with you in that outfit!" ◆ "Hey, thanks. I'll come back right after supper. Remember, we're supposed to meet everyone at six," Ellen said as she ran out the door.

◆ Just before six o'clock, Ellen rang Sebastian's doorbell once more. ◆ "My goodness," his mother said, seeing the costume for the first time. "I bet people will put extra money in your UNICEF box when they see that getup!" With that, she handed Ellen and Sebastian each a bright orange UNICEF box and a big trick-or-treat bag. ◆ "Thanks, Mom. You can have all my gumdrops and jelly beans!" Sebastian said with a smile. They all knew that he didn't like gumdrops and jelly beans, so it was an easy offer for him to make. ◆ The two of them rushed out to meet some of their other friends from Havens School, and then the whole group of eight boys and girls who had been trick-or-treating together for years headed out. ◆ "Trick-or-treat for UNICEF!" they called out at the first house. A woman dressed as a witch opened the door and tossed candy bars into their bags and dimes into their boxes. Not bad for the first house. ◆ On they went until the bags were heavy and their boxes jingled with coins. ◆ "Come on over to my house and let's see what we got!" Ellen invited. ◆ "Okay. I just have to stop by and ask my mom," Sebastian replied. His mom said fine, so the two of them went to Ellen's room and spread out their candy on the floor. There were piles and piles of it. Then they shook the money in their UNICEF boxes. The boxes felt quite full. Not bad! ◆ Sebastian started to read the information on the back of the boxes that told how much their money would buy. ◆ "It says that $10 will buy breakfast for all the children at a school for a month!" he said. "Imagine, a whole month! Or $10 will immunize a child against the six childhood diseases—or buy a family new farm tools that will make their work much easier. You sure can get a lot with only a little money. Hey, it says here that a well for a whole village, which would give them clean, healthy water, only costs $200— $200! My Nintendo and game cartridges cost more than that!" ◆ That night as her mother was tucking her in bed, Ellen asked, "Mom, do you ever feel bad that some people are hungry, and others, like us, have so much?" ◆ "Well, yes. I wish it wasn't that way," she said. ◆ "It's not fair. I wish I could help them," Ellen said. ◆ "Maybe you can," her mother said, kissing her on the forehead. "Good night, dear. Sleep well." ◆ "'Night, Mom." ◆ The next day in school, it was as if the teacher had been listening in on Ellen's dreams. On the board was a big chart for each of them to write down how much they had collected for UNICEF. When they added it all up it came to $118. Ellen and Sebastian exchanged glances across the room. More than half the cost of a well! ◆ Then the teacher did a really amazing thing. She brought in the television set and showed them a movie about an African village getting a well. It was even better than Ellen and Sebastian had imagined. A well helped in so many ways. ◆ "It's great that the women and girls didn't have to walk so far to get water anymore," Ellen said. "But I don't think it was fair that the boys didn't have to help." ◆ "Me either," Sebastian said. "I couldn't believe how much time they had to spend every single day, just getting water." ◆ "Yeah, and then they got sick from drinking it!" someone else chimed in. "They must be sick half the time." ◆ "In some places, they are," their teacher told them. "That's why wells are so important. Wouldn't it be great if we could send enough money for a village to get a well?" ◆ "Yes!" they all said at once. ◆ And so they started a project. After brainstorming different ways they could raise money, the class broke into groups. Sebastian was in the group that was figuring out what odd jobs they could do. Ellen's group was deciding between an all-school garage sale and a bake sale. Another group planned a walk-a-thon. ◆ For a month the class turned into "Ending Hunger Central," and most of their schoolwork centered around raising the money and learning about the difference it would make. ◆ Everyone in the class picked an odd job on the list and earned money doing it. Sebastian's group held a car wash near the school one Saturday. Ellen's group spent one Saturday knocking on doors and offering to rake leaves in people's yards. One man gave them $10 and it wasn't even a big yard! ◆ The bake sale group got permission to sell things one day after school. They made posters for each classroom, and one for the front hall of the school, announcing the sale and what it was for. The posters reminded people to bring money to buy things. It was a big hit. Especially the chocolate–chocolate chip cookies that Carlos and his mom baked. ◆ They decided to hold the walk-a-thon on the weekend before Thanksgiving. They wanted to remind everyone about all they had to be thankful for. Every sponsor got a copy of the class newspaper they had created about world hunger and what each person can do to end it. Each student in the class contributed to the paper. Some wrote poems, others wrote news stories, and others wrote stories about the World Summit for Children and ORS. Ellen's poem and picture about a world with no hunger were on the back cover. The walk-a-thon turned out to be a big success, with kids from other classes joining in. They had 40 walkers and over 150 sponsors. ◆ By Thanksgiving they had raised far more than the $200 for one well. But they didn't want to stop. The whole class voted to continue activities to end hunger until school was out for the summer. ◆ Throughout the year they raised money and studied about hunger. They invited people who'd been to places where hungry people lived to come talk to them. They read about hunger in America, and some of the students volunteered to serve meals at a homeless shelter. They were surprised to learn that so many hungry people lived right nearby, and they decided to give some of the money they raised to help them, too. ◆ In May, they heard from the first village they had sent money to. The village had a new well, and the leftover money had bought school supplies and breakfasts for all the children. Ellen and her classmates had also written letters to the children when they sent their donation, and had received one back from the whole school to their class, thanking them for everything and asking lots of questions about life in America. ◆ To finish the whole thing off, in June, before school was out, they had an Ending Hunger Day for the entire school. They invited their parents to the assembly. Sebastian gave a speech about how a little money could make a big difference, and Ellen was an African woman in a play about giving shots to village children to prevent disease. ◆ On the last day of school, the class added up all the money they'd raised and everything they had been able to do with it. All together it came to just under $2,000. ◆ "Wow!" the kids said to one another. "Unbelievable!" ◆ Ellen looked at Sebastian, with a grin on her face. "Just wait 'til next year!" she whispered. ◆◆

50 Things
Kids Can Do
to End Hunger

What Kinds of Things Will Make a Difference?

Here are some of the kinds of things that people—kids or adults—who want to end hunger can do. See which kinds appeal to you. Maybe one or two, or maybe all of them!

- **Find out**. Learn about hunger, and what life with hunger is like. Find out about the promises to end hunger that the leaders of almost every country on earth recently made at the World Summit for Children.

- **Speak out.** Help others learn as well. Give kids and adults the facts about what is needed now—and ask them to get involved, to take action, to make ending hunger their business. Let them know that if they want to save the earth, they need to save the people on it as well. Use the media—newspapers, magazines, radio, and TV—to help spread the word.

- **Write.** Let your government officials know how you feel. Governments spend a lot of money on what the people who vote for them think is important. Write to the people who make the laws in your country—people in government. Ask them to pass laws that will help keep 40,000 children from dying of hunger and preventable sickness every day, laws that will give millions of other children a chance to enjoy the gift that life is.

Tell them that you want them to be serious about the United Nations Convention on the Rights of the Child, and to pass the laws that will protect children from hunger in your country, and that will help other countries do the same.

A letter from a child will get attention.

So would a visit to a government official's office.

- **Give money.** Support the people and organizations who are working to help the hungry people end their own hunger. These are the ones that feed and care for the hungry now and help them improve their lives so that they can feed themselves. They are the ones that are letting the world know about hunger so that everyone will take an active part in ending it.

  Their work keeps millions of kids and adults alive and gives millions of others a chance to have healthy lives. Giving money to, and raising money for, these organizations is one of the best ways to help end hunger.

- **Help the hungry where you live.** In every country in the world there are some hungry people.

  Sometimes the people who go hungry live in our own neighborhood. Draw attention to, and help feed, the hungry people living near you.

  Urge the leaders in your community to work together to end hunger where you live.

- **Come up with your own ideas of what to do.** When you get excited about ending hunger, about getting **everyone** involved in ending it, you will probably find that you and your friends have some great new ideas of your own that you want to try.

  Do them!

On the next pages are 50 ideas for projects and activities that you can do, and how to do them.

And don't forget—it's fine to have fun while you're helping to end world hunger!

Things You Can Do

1. Give a talk.
2. Send a cow.
3. Hold a "no-food" dinner.
4. "Adopt" a child in a hungry country.
5. Talk on the radio.
6. Get your family involved.
7. Stop_____! (Fill in the blank.)
8. Write a story or an article on hunger.
9. Make a video.
10. Get people's attention by fasting.
11. Get a rock star or movie star excited about ending hunger.
12. Volunteer.
13. Write letters to officials in government.
14. Feed someone today.
15. Send thank-you notes for the end of hunger.
16. Be an artist for the end of hunger.
17. Celebrate World Food Day.
18. Hold the hamburger.
19. Make an Ending Hunger scrapbook.

Things to Do at School

20. Join Save the Children's "School to School" program.
21. Hold a schoolwide Ending Hunger art contest.
22. Buy a well.
23. Join RESULTS.
24. Put together an Ending Hunger newspaper.
25. Find out for real: Where are the hungry? Where is the food?
26. Have your class sponsor a project in a hungry country.
27. Draw comics for the end of hunger.
28. Put on a puppet show or skit.

29. Organize a supermarket food drive.
30. Trick-or-treat for UNICEF.
31. Learn a lot more.
32. Organize an Ending Hunger Sabbath.
33. Take part in Valentine Vision.
34. Hold a world hunger banquet.
35. Start a Youth Ending Hunger club.
36. Make Ending Hunger coloring books.
37. Sing!
38. Invite a speaker from a hunger organization.
39. Hold a Hunger Awareness Week at your school.

Ways to Raise Money

40. Recycle for the end of hunger.
41. Hold a "Something-a-thon" for the end of hunger.
42. Earn money.
43. Buy and sell UNICEF cards.
44. Participate in Oxfam's Fast for a World Harvest.
45. Hold a fundraising event.
46. Clown Around for Kids.
47. Organize a World Map-a-thon.
48. Hold a CROP Walk.
49. Hold a community cleanup for the end of hunger.
50. Just ask for it!

On pages 158–166 you can find the telephone numbers and addresses of the groups mentioned.

1. Give a talk.

Give a talk on hunger to some friends, your class, another class, a school assembly, or even to some adults. Tell them what you know about the lives of hungry children. Let them know that hunger can be ended. Tell them about the two kinds of hunger—famine and chronic hunger—and about the World Summit for Children. Mention that if we are interested in ecology and saving the earth, we need to take care of the hungry people. Don't be shy. This is important—and people want to know!

And don't forget the kindergartners or other little kids! Offer to go into the classes in your school and tell them or read them stories about ending hunger. You would be surprised at how interested they are! You could also tell them about the "I Can See" penny collection project described on page 74. Afterwards, give them a chance to draw pictures about what they have learned.

Tell them:

- Your name and what you are going to talk about (ending hunger) and why you have come to talk with them.

- Why you think kids can make a difference in ending hunger.

- The facts:

  27 children die every minute.

  40,000 children die every day, mostly from hunger and preventable sickness.

Millions of others suffer from hunger every day of their lives.

- There is enough food already. (Most kids and grown-ups don't know this.) All those people, mostly children, are dying when there is enough food to feed everyone! That is the tragedy.

- Ending hunger helps us save the earth and have world peace. (See pages 6–7 to help you explain how this works.)

- If enough people get involved in ending hunger, we can end it! World leaders of almost every country have already promised to end the hunger of children in their countries.

- To end hunger would cost about the same amount of money as the world spends on cigarettes and tobacco every two months!

- Kids can help by talking about it, writing about it, drawing about it, and by spreading the word that hunger can be ended—and that it is up to us to make it happen.

- Kids can also help by giving money and asking other people to give money to the groups that are helping hungry people.

- The main thing is: tell lots of people the facts about ending hunger, and ask them to please get involved.

- Share with them some of your favorite ideas or projects that kids can do, to get them into action.

2. Send a cow. Remember how great it was for the Indian children in the story on page 61 to get a calf for their village? You can send a cow to a family or to a village. A cow gives them milk to drink, and maybe even lets them earn money by selling extra milk. Or you can send a family of rabbits for the villagers to raise for food. On page 161 you will find the address of the Heifer Project International, a group that sends animals to help villagers.

3. Hold a "no-food" dinner.

Get your family really interested in ending hunger. If they are brave enough, hold a no-food dinner. You could just serve water for dinner, and during the time saved from not cooking, setting the table, eating, or cleaning up, talk to them about ending hunger and read sections from this book or other information on ending hunger to them. You could let them know that hungry families are very much like your own—except that they live where they cannot feed themselves, no matter how hard they work. You could read them the exercise on pages 12–13.

Together you could choose the group you all want to send money to—the money that was saved from dinner that night!

4. "Adopt" a foster child in a hungry country.

This doesn't mean the child comes and lives with you. How it works is your family (or club or Scout troop or anyone) sends around $20 a month to support a child to make sure he or she has enough to eat and that basic needs are taken care of. Some of the groups will send you a picture of your "adopted" brother or sister, and you'll get letters from him or her as well.

These are some of the groups that help you sponsor foster children around the world. Their addresses and telephone numbers are on pages 159–164.

- Children's Aid International
- Christian Children's Fund
- Plan International USA
- Save the Children

5. Talk on the radio.

We know that the more people involved in ending hunger, the better. One great way to let people know about it is by radio. People with radio programs are often looking for things to talk about and guest speakers.

If you know anyone who works at a radio station (or if you feel brave enough to give your favorite station a call), offer yourself as a guest speaker. Or ask to speak to the program manager and suggest that he or she make ending hunger a topic on one of the talk shows. You could also ask them to air a public service announcement (PSA) that tells people about the different kinds of hunger, about the World Summit for Children, and what is needed to end hunger. PSAs are short (15-, 30-, or 45-second) announcements on the radio. Who knows—they might even let you record the announcement!

SAMPLE 15-SECOND PUBLIC SERVICE ANNOUNCEMENT (PSA)

40,000 children die of hunger and preventable diseases every day.

Needlessly.

Hunger can be ended—if enough people get involved.

Please—support the hunger organizations of your choice.

If you are the courageous type, don't call or write—just get someone to drive you to the radio station—and walk in! Tell them what you want and why!

6. Get your family involved.

Most likely, you have some pretty smart and talented members in your family. Help them find out what *they* can do.

One thing you could all do together is to use holidays as a time to give money to help end hunger. For instance, instead of, or in addition to, giving Christmas or Hanukkah presents this year, maybe your family could make a donation to some organization that you want to help, in honor of all the people you would have given presents to. During the holidays you could make and send cards that say something like:

> "In celebration of _____ (fill in the holiday or special occasion) we have made a contribution to _____ (name of the organization) in your name because we love you, and we want to end hunger in this world."
>
> (signed) The _____ Family

You could do the same for birthdays, Valentine's Day, graduation, new babies, anniversaries—any time!

Does your mom or dad work with other people? Maybe your parents' businesses or your friends' parents' businesses would like to help. You could ask them to make a donation to some organizations that are working on ending hunger. You will need to know about the different organizations, and how to contact them, so that once the grown-ups say yes, you can make sure they know where to send their money. (Descriptions of hunger organizations are on pages 158–166, including addresses.) Some adults like to share some of their money every month with people who are poor or hungry. This is called **tithing**. Kids could tithe, too, with allowance or baby-sitting money. Want to give it a try?

If you have older brothers or sisters, see if they would be interested in getting the high school kids involved.

7. **Stop** _____ ! (Fill in the blank.) Think of something you want to stop doing—say, biting your nails, or forgetting to make your bed, or fighting with your brother or sister— whatever you want to stop.

Then make a deal with the people in your family. For

every week (or time) you Stop! doing the thing, they agree to contribute a certain amount of money to help end hunger.

Depending on how many things you want to Stop!, you could earn quite a bit of money this way. Remember, even small amounts of money can save children's lives. Just make sure the arrangement doesn't turn into some kind of bribe, or where you ask to be paid to do what is your responsibility anyway. Ideally this activity should benefit everybody: you, your family, and the hungry children. Check it out!

8. Write a story or an article on hunger. Write a story about the life of some hungry children. Draw pictures and really do an excellent job with it.

Then write or call the editor of your local newspaper and tell him or her that you would like them to print your story. Or offer to be interviewed about ending hunger. Or you could offer to help give them facts about chronic hunger and famine and the Convention on the Rights of the Child so they could write their own article.

If you were an editor, wouldn't you pay attention if some kid called you to tell you about an important story that you should put in your paper?

It may seem awfully scary or hard to do—but you said you wanted to help end hunger. This is the kind of thing that will help!

Another good thing to do is to write a letter to the editor. Most newspapers have a section where they print letters that people send in. Anyone is allowed to write. If the editor decides to print your letter, a lot of people in your area will find out about the kids who are hungry. You can find your newspaper's address on the Letters to the Editor page of the paper. (Of course, it would be great if your friends or classmates got involved in writing letters. The more letters the editor receives, the more he or she will realize that people are serious about ending hunger.)

9. Make a video.
Talk some older kids into helping you make a video about famine and chronic hunger or something else you have learned about ending hunger. Or a group of you could act out one of the stories in this or another book.

Offer to show your video at school, to your parents' friends, to your friends, to the Scouts, to Sunday school classes, to the PTA.

If there is a community cable TV station where you live, they might be willing to air it, plus maybe interview you as well.

Another way you could go is to borrow videos about ending hunger and look at them at home or take them to school. They are either free or cost very little to rent. A list of some videos on ending hunger begins on page 169.

10. Get people's attention by fasting.
Have you ever tried fasting? Fasting means not eating—on purpose. It wouldn't be smart to do it for too long, but it's fine to miss a meal or two if you want to try to fast.

Get your parents' permission first and decide how many meals you will fast for: one, two, or even all the meals for a day. As your stomach complains, allow yourself to think of the kids who feel like that all the time.

If people ask you why you are not eating, tell them that you are taking ending hunger seriously. Let them know why! Invite them to get involved!

Another thing you could do is to limit your food, for a day

or even two, to the kind and amount of food that children who are chronically hungry get. It won't hurt you for a day or two. For example, maybe you would have some plain rice and tea for breakfast, a corn tortilla with some beans on it for lunch, and some watered-down soup and rice for supper. See whether your friends or family would be interested in joining you.

If you have ordered any of the free materials that hunger organizations make available to kids (see page 158) it would be good to review them before your day of fasting. In that way you will be able to educate the people who ask about your fast or your simple meals.

You can send the money your family would have spent on your food that day to a group working on ending hunger.

11. **Get a rock star or movie star excited about ending hunger.** Have you ever noticed how much attention people pay to what movie stars and rock stars are doing and saying? Wouldn't it be great if they used their fame to get people involved in ending hunger for the children of the world—and for everyone?

Write a letter to your favorite movie or TV stars or musicians and let them know about the two kinds of hunger, and the World Summit for Children. Ask them to use their concerts or shows or interviews to let the world know that they care about ending hunger—and to ask their audiences to get involved. Some stars are already interested in ending world hunger. (Ask your parents or teachers about BandAid, USA for Africa, or Live Aid, for example.) Others are really interested in saving the earth. You could tell them about the connection between saving the earth and ending hunger.

You can find out where to send your letter by checking *Celebrity Access* by Thomas Burford, *The Address Book* by Michael Levine, or *Who's Who*, or ask the librarian to help you find the addresses you need.

12. Volunteer.
Find out what the volunteer agencies that are feeding the hungry in your area are doing, and offer to help out some weekend day or after school. Most communities have a whole range of programs to help feed the hungry locally. You might get to help prepare food in a soup kitchen, pack grocery bags at a food bank, answer telephones or send out mailings in an office—who knows? Call the United Way (their telephone number is in the white pages of the phone book) to find out which groups are helping the hungry near where you live. This would be fun to do with a couple of friends and your mom or dad or any other adult who would like to join you.

13. Write letters to government officials.
You could write to the president or to your senator or representative and tell them that you are a child and that it is not all right with you that 40,000 children are dying every day in our world, mostly from hunger, and that millions are suffering from hunger right now. Ask them to pass laws that will help end hunger.

Here's how to reach some of them. Your friendly librarian can help you find the names and addresses of your senator, representative, and local government officials.

ADDRESSES OF THE U.S. PRESIDENT, SENATORS, AND REPRESENTATIVES

PRESIDENT OF THE UNITED STATES
OF AMERICA

(President's name)
The White House
1600 Pennsylvania Ave. NW
Washington, DC 20500
Begin: Dear Mr. or Ms. President

SENATOR OR REPRESENTATIVE

Senator:
The Honorable (Name)
United States Senate
Washington, DC 20501
Begin: Dear Senator (Name)

Representative:
The Honorable (Name)
United States House of Representatives
Washington, DC 20501
Begin: Dear Representative (Name)

THE LEADER OF ANOTHER COUNTRY

Name, title
_____ Embassy
The United Nations
United Nations Plaza
New York, NY 10017
Begin: (Use his or her title)

Here are two sample letters. See which one you think would work better. (Of course, you don't have to use either one —you can come up with your own letter.)

SAMPLE LETTER #1

Hey You!
You folks should pay attention to hunger, you meanies. If you are so smart, how come so many kids are dying? Aren't you ashamed of yourself?
Don't count on me to vote for you when I get old enough to vote!

Signed, XXXX

SAMPLE LETTER #2

Dear (Person's name and title, if he or she has one),
I hope you will pay attention to this letter because it is about something that is really important to me and the world: 40,000 kids are dying every day. Millions and millions of others are suffering from hunger. I am a kid myself, so I really hate that idea.
It would be so great if you could help out. If you need to know some of the facts, I can help you out, since I have been learning about ending hunger.
Please think seriously about this problem and about what you can do about it.

Thanks a lot.

Sincerely, XXX

14. Feed someone today.

Many of us live where there are homeless and hungry people. You can give them something to eat, just like that. You don't need to wait. Make a peanut butter sandwich. Make two. Make some lunches, put them in brown paper bags, and ask your mom or dad to take you to where there are people who are hungry. Tell your mom or dad what you want to do, and ask their support. Who knows? You might end up like Trevor, the boy mentioned on page 19. He started bringing some food and blankets to the homeless where he lived, and now there is a whole organization doing just that.

In fact, if every kid who reads this book went out and fed one, two, three hungry people—what do you suppose would happen?

15. Send thank-you notes for the end of hunger.

Here's a kind of thank-you note different from the one you write to thank Aunt Nina for your birthday sweater.

You'll need to pay attention to the news, either on TV or in the paper, to pull this off. Watch the news for anyone who is doing something about ending hunger. It could be a rock star who is giving a concert to benefit famine victims, it could be a politician who is trying to pass a law to help the hungry where you live, it could be a TV show where they talk about the World Summit for Children and the rights of children. Then send them a thank-you note! Your neighborhood librarian can help you find out where to send it. Let them know that you noticed what they did, and on behalf of the hungry children of the world, thank them for their action. That would probably surprise them—and maybe encourage them to keep doing more!

16. Be an artist for the end of hunger.

Put the end of hunger into your artwork. You can make up designs, draw pictures of hungry kids, or kids helping kids, or a world without hunger. Doodle the end of hunger while you are on the phone!

You could also make a big banner or sign or poster or mural that shows what you believe about hunger—what you really feel about the fact that there are kids dying of hunger in a world that has enough food to feed everyone. Invite some kids over to work on it with you, if you like. Then find some great places to hang it. The living room. Your classroom. The halls at school. The public library. The dry cleaner's. Your mom's or dad's office. Your bedroom. The mayor's office!

17. Celebrate World Food Day.

World Food Day is October 16. On that day all around the world people celebrate the glories of our rich and beautiful planet.

It's a great day to hold some kind of activity. If you write to the World Food Day Committee, 1001 22nd St. NW, Washington, DC 20437, they will send you free tons of great ideas on what you and the kids in your school can do.

There are a number of special days and events each year that have to do with ending hunger. The organizations that put them on love it when kids participate. On pages 181–183 is a calendar that lists some of the major ones. Copy the dates onto your family calendar, and invite friends and family and schoolmates to celebrate some of the ending-hunger events when they are coming up. Contact the organization putting on the event a few weeks in advance to get all the details.

18. Hold the hamburger.

Next time you go to a fast-food restaurant and order a hamburger, ask them to "hold the meat." (When you ask the person taking your order in a restaurant to "hold" something, it means you don't want that thing—they should keep it in the kitchen!)

Here is why:

Meat comes from cows. Cows eat a lot of grain. It takes a lot of land to grow the grain to feed the cows. If the land weren't being used to graze the cows, hungry families might be able to use it to grow vegetables on. Cows also drink a lot of water that could be used to water crops. Of course, your one measly hamburger won't end up feeding someone who is hungry, but still it is good to know that if people cut down on the amount of meat they ate, they would help make more food available.

19. Make an Ending Hunger Scrapbook.

Start noticing when hunger is discussed in the newspaper, in magazines, on TV, and on the radio. If you like collecting things, make an Ending Hunger scrapbook. Buy or make a scrapbook and then start cutting out articles.

Here's the trick: See if you can find the articles about **ending** hunger, not about what a horrible problem hunger is. Often when newspapers write about hunger, they make it seem awful and hopeless, so people are left feeling that nothing can be done about it.

You could have two sections to your scrapbook. One could be called "Hunger" and in it you would put the articles on how bad it is, the tragedies, the famines, all the really depressing stuff. In the other section you could put articles that talk about new ways to end hunger, children who are being saved, countries that are achieving the goals of the

World Summit for Children, new discoveries about foods or plants that could feed the planet—things like that. It will be interesting to see which part of the scrapbook grows faster. In any case, by collecting and reading all the articles yourself, you will soon become very well educated on the subject.

20. Join Save the Children's "School to School" program.

Your class or school can adopt a school in Africa or Asia or the Caribbean. (Check a map to see where these areas are.) The way it works is that your school raises money to help the kids in a school in one of those places. The money is spent on school supplies for your sister school or even to build a new classroom. Do you think the kids in your school would go for the idea?

21. Hold a schoolwide Ending Hunger art contest. Start off by giving a short talk in your class about ending hunger. If your class has been studying hunger, maybe you could offer to go around to the other classes and give talks, letting them know about the contest. Or you could even get all the schools in your district to participate.

You could call it a "World Without Hunger" poster contest, or the "Ending Hunger Symbol" contest, or any name you like. The contestants try to make a poster or design a symbol that gets people involved in taking **action** to end hunger. They could design a new symbol for ending hunger.

(You've seen the "No Smoking" symbol—the picture of a cigarette in a red circle, with a line through it.)

Ask your principal whether you can display the posters and symbols in the halls, in the lunchroom, in the library, or wherever there is room in your school.

You get to decide who the judges will be. As for prizes, you or some of your friends or someone's mother or father could invite some storekeepers or restaurant owners near you to donate some. Bet you they say yes! Storekeepers and restaurant owners want hunger to end, too!

Afterwards it might be possible to pick 12 of the best posters and put them into an Ending Hunger calendar that the kids could sell, or make them into buttons or stickers. They could really help spread the message and could be used to raise funds as well.

22. Buy a well.
Millions of children could be saved each year if only they were able to get clean water instead of water that makes them sick. Buy a well that will give safe water to a whole village in Africa by sending money to UNICEF, Save the Children, IDEX, CARE, or Africare. (Look on pages 158–166 to see how to contact them.) Read on for some ideas on how to raise money to buy a well for a village.

23. Join RESULTS.
You can join a letter-writing group called RESULTS (236 Massachusetts Ave. NE, Washington, DC 20002-4980).

When you (and your family or friends or class) join, the organization lets you know what letters would make a difference now, whom to write to, what the issues are, and where to send the letters. For example, they know which laws the government is thinking about passing that could help hungry people.

They also have a "Keeping the Promise" campaign and materials, to help us see how to support lawmakers in keeping the promises made at the World Summit for Children.

24. Put together an Ending Hunger newspaper.

After learning about ending hunger, your class could put together a class newspaper. You could call it something like the *Ending Hunger News.*

You could catch everyone's attention with a big "40,000 KIDS DIED OF HUNGER TODAY" headline; articles on some of the facts; stories about kids who are hungry; cartoons about the two kinds of hunger; interviews; charts and maps; and a special "What Kids Can Do" section. Sharing your newspaper with the rest of the school would be a good way to get them interested.

25. Find out for real: Where are the hungry? Where is the food? This activity doesn't really end hunger. But it may change the way you think about it for the rest of your life.

It takes some preparation, but is really interesting. See if your mom or dad or older brother or sister can come to your classroom to help out. Naturally, you'll need to get your teacher's permission ahead of time. The activity will take about 30 minutes. Here's what you do:

- Bring in (or pull down) a map of the world.

- Talk a little about some of the things you have learned about hunger, how many kids are dying (could the class guess before you told them?), how something like measles or a cold can kill hungry kids—things like that.

- Then tell the class that you would like to do a demonstration with them so they can see for themselves where the people in the world live, and who gets how much food.

- You will need to divide the class up into five groups. Ahead of time, write the name of each group in large letters on a piece of paper. These are the groups:

  SOUTH AMERICA
  AFRICA AND THE MIDDLE EAST
  EUROPE AND SOVIET COUNTRIES
  NORTH AMERICA
  ASIA

(If you don't know where those areas of the world are yourself, stop here and check a map or globe so you will know in advance!)

- Tell your classmates that you are now going to divide them the way the population of the world is really divided. One at a time, read out the names and ask whether anyone has ever traveled there, or has family from there, and then choose the right number of kids to be in that group. They should get out of their seats and gather in their group, holding the sign.

- The numbers below work if there are 35 kids in your class. (The percentages are in parentheses in case you need to know how to divide a bigger or smaller class.)

SOUTH AMERICA	3 children (9%)
AFRICA AND THE MIDDLE EAST	4 children (11%)
EUROPE AND SOVIET COUNTRIES	6 children (17%)
NORTH AMERICA	2 children (6%)
ASIA	20 children (57%)

- Once everyone is in groups, it will be pretty clear to everyone where most of the people in our world live!

- Now let them know that you are going to pass out food— something like Teddy Grahams or small cookies or M&Ms works very well for this—and that you will be dividing it among the groups the way the food in our world is really divided.

- Ask them not to eat or touch the cookies, and with a helper, deliver this number of cookies to the groups:

SOUTH AMERICA	3 cookies (6%)
AFRICA AND THE MIDDLE EAST	1 cookie (2%)
EUROPE AND SOVIET COUNTRIES	23 cookies (45%)
NORTH AMERICA	15 cookies (29%)
ASIA	9 cookies (18%)

People may not like how unfair it seems. Tell them that, like it or not, that's how it really is. (By the way, it is fine to let them know that after the demonstration you are going to share the treats equally.)

With your teacher's help, hold a discussion about the situation in the world.

In fact, this activity may be a good one to get the kids interested in taking on some of the projects you have been reading about in this book!

26. Have your class sponsor a project in a hungry country.

Get in touch with IDEX or Lasting Links to find a project you or your class wants to support in another country. These organizations match schools or other groups with the particular projects that interest them. IDEX will also send your school an educational kit so you can learn about the country and area you are supporting. Your money might help finish building a school in Zimbabwe, start a kindergarten in Tibet, start a small soap-making cooperative in the Philippines, set up a medical clinic in Burkina Faso, or start a garden project in Nicaragua. The group will give you all the details. The addresses of both organizations are in the list starting on page 158.

Lots of organizations sponsor projects your class can support, depending on how much money you raise. Most of the organizations listed in the "Resources" section can tell you about the projects they need funds for and you can pick what you like: buying goats, sewing machines, wells, school supplies, seeds—you name it!

27. Draw comics for the end of hunger.

You know how much kids like comics! Invite other kids to make a cartoon or comic book out of some of the messages or information from this book. Just because it is an important subject doesn't mean we have to be all serious about it! Maybe the kids in your class could come up with ways to show some of the facts, ways that get other kids interested.

You could put your cartoons or comics in your school newspaper, on the bulletin boards, or ask the neighborhood librarian whether you can put them up in the public library.

28. Put on a puppet show or skit.

Put on a puppet show or skit about chronic hunger and famine or about the Convention on the Rights of the Child. Your puppets or characters could be in simple costumes. Try to help people see how the problem can be solved rather than just making them feel bad about how many kids are sick and dying from hunger. See whether you can show that the hungry are hardworking, loving people—like the people in your audience. Show that the problem is that they are not able to grow enough food or earn enough money to buy enough food to feed their families.

29. Organize a supermarket food drive.

A supermarket food drive takes some organizing, but can be a lot of fun, and can end up collecting quite a bit of food for the hungry in your area. In a supermarket food drive, shoppers are asked to buy one or two extra things when they are doing their grocery shopping on a certain day. You and your friends are there to collect the food and take it to a group that is feeding the hungry near where you live. Here is how it works:

- With a parent or teacher, enroll the manager of the grocery store in your idea. Explain that you and your friends or classmates or club members would like to put up posters ahead of time to let the shoppers know that the food drive is coming. (Pick a Saturday, or another day when you don't have school.)

- If the whole class is going to participate, organize yourselves into teams. On the day of the food drive, some of you stand at the entrance handing out a list of most-needed items to shoppers as they enter the store; others of you stand with big cardboard boxes at the cash registers or right outside the store to collect the food.

- Some adult is needed to deliver all the food to the agency that feeds hungry people near where you live.

- Part of the preparation will be finding out about hunger in your area, which organizations are doing what, and what foods they especially need. The United Way can give you the names and phone numbers.

30. Trick-or-treat for UNICEF.

Thousands and thousands of kids around the United States use Halloween as a time to raise money to help hungry kids. The story on pages 99–106 shows how trick-or-treating for UNICEF can work and how much fun it can be. Lots of kids trick-or-treat for UNICEF, but not so many know where the money goes and what it buys. If they did, they probably would collect a lot more!

You can let them know that every 10 cents buys an ORS packet (see page 96 to find out about ORS); every 2 cents buys a Vitamin A pill that can keep a child from going blind; and every $10 buys vaccine to immunize a child, which will very likely save his or her life! Contact UNICEF for free collection boxes.

Have a contest this year to see which class can collect the most money.

31. Learn a lot more.

Learn a lot more. Next time you need to do a report in school, how about picking a subject that will give you more information about ending hunger?

Here are some possible topics:

- What is food anyway, and why is it so important? Ask your teacher whether you can do a unit on food. Find out what makes something food. For example, blood or pigs' heads may be considered food by some people in Asia, but you probably wouldn't agree. What's so important about good food and balanced diets? Any chance you might be malnourished? (Hint: Include some research on junk food and the scientists who claim people living in North America are malnourished.)

- Infant mortality and under-five mortality rates—what are they and what difference do they make? Why is the Population Data Sheet that the Population Resource Bureau publishes so important?

- What on earth is GOBI? ORS? Find out more about these life-saving programs

- How did the World Summit for Children come to be? What are the Rights of the Child? How many countries have made the rights of children laws?

- What is InterAction, the "umbrella" organization for groups working on ending hunger in the United States? What is it for, what has it accomplished, what does it need?

- Find out about water. How many people are without clean water, and what does that have to do with ending hunger? Hint: This is a very important subject. Some people say that most of the deaths from hunger could be avoided completely if children were able to drink safe water.

- The Child Survival Campaign is one of the greatest things happening in ending hunger these days. Find out more about it and how the kids in your school can support it.

- How are ending hunger and saving the earth connected? How does one help the other, and vice versa?

Your school librarian or the librarian in the public library can get you started on any of these topics.

32. Organize an Ending Hunger Sabbath.

Sabbath means holy day, or the day a person goes to church or temple. Once the kids in your class are involved in ending hunger, pick some weekend and see if you can have everybody's minister or priest or rabbi or holy person talk about ending hunger that weekend. (Show them the "Resources" section of this book if they would like to know what to read to educate themselves before they speak.) It would be great to know that during that weekend the people in your town were going to get to hear about the importance of getting involved in ending hunger, no matter where they went to church or temple. The organization RESULTS can send you ideas about what the Ending Hunger Sabbath can include. (Their address is on page 164.)

Could **kids** really pull off such a thing, getting all the churches and temples in your area involved on a particular weekend? Definitely! You will be surprised at how much you and your friends can accomplish if you aren't shy and just jump in!

You could also show this book to your Sunday school teacher, who might find some activities he or she would love to do with the class.

33. Take part in Valentine Vision.

On February 14 children all around the world share a moment of silence while they imagine a world without hunger. They also make valentines for hungry children in other countries, showing their love for them. Contact Valentine Vision, 78 Summer St., Weston, MA 02193, to find out how you can send your valentines this year to children who are hungry, and how to join in the moment of silence.

34. Hold a world hunger banquet.

Here is an activity that could be done in your class, and is even better if a large group takes it on. It involves some preparation and you will need some adults' support, but it is definitely worth doing. Here's what you do:

Let the kids in your class know in advance that you'll be doing a special activity. Ask your parents or some of the other parents to help out. Arrange to have lunch in the classroom on this day if it's at all possible. If it isn't, do the activity right before lunch, when the kids are the hungriest.

When the kids come to school in the morning, have each child reach into a box where they cannot see inside and pull out a "meal ticket." Tell them not to lose it. For a class of 35, make 8 blue tickets, 19 yellow tickets, and 8 red ones. (If your class is bigger or smaller than 35, adjust the numbers. Your teacher can help you figure it out.)

You will need to prepare three different lunches or snacks in advance:

- One of them, for 8 people, should be very fancy and very delicious. Serve chocolate milk and ice cream, maybe pizza or hamburgers or something everyone loves. There should be plenty of food. If possible, use china plates, and even have a tablecloth and flowers for the table.

- Another lunch, for 19 people, should be quite simple, such as a plain bowl of rice with some vegetables. The kids can sit at desks to eat.

- The last lunch, also for 8, should be some warm water and a very small serving of rice. The people eating that meal should sit on the floor.

When lunchtime comes, set out the lunches and announce to the kids that you are going to have a lunch that shows how much people around the world get to eat. Point out that in fact, some people on the earth have plenty to eat, and others go hungry. Invite the kids with the blue tickets to the fancy meal. Invite the kids with the yellow tickets to the plain meal. Invite the kids with the red tickets to eat their meager meal on the floor. (Please be careful not to hurt anyone's feelings here. If you think it wise, you may want to have extra treats for everyone for when the activity is finished.)

After the meal, have a discussion about how each group felt. Point out during the discussion that in fact, we do have enough food to feed everyone in the world. However, the way the world works is that not everyone has what is needed to stay alive or stay healthy.

Large groups of adults have done this activity, and it has been really successful. In fact, not long ago Oxfam America invited a bunch of celebrities to world hunger banquets. They sold tickets to the banquets, and they didn't mention anything in advance about how the food was going to be organized! Newspapers all over the world covered the events.

No matter who does this activity, the discussion afterwards is one of the most important parts of the experience.

35. Start a Youth Ending Hunger club.

Sometimes it's easier to get things started when you are doing it with a few friends. Start an ending-hunger club with some of your friends. Together you can take on some of the projects in this book, and come up with lots more that you feel like doing. Youth Ending Hunger is a worldwide movement of kids who form YEH clubs. YEH members have ridden their bikes across the country, met with world leaders, been on TV, and raised hundreds of thousands of dollars, all for ending hunger. Contact the Hunger Project, YEH, 1388 Sutter St., San Francisco, CA 94109, to get a starter kit and to find out how to begin a Youth Ending Hunger club.

36. Make Ending Hunger coloring books. Make coloring books for the kids in the younger grades at your school. Have the kids who like art draw some of the things you've learned about ending hunger. Others of you can write the little sentences or phrases to go underneath.

Find a way to get them duplicated; surely there is someone who would help you out. Take your coloring books to the younger classes (start by going to your favorite teacher's class), talk to them about hunger, and pass out the books. They will love them!

37. Sing! Instead of telling people about ending hunger— sing it to them! Take this song to your music teacher or anyone who can read music. It has a great melody and can be sung as a round. Maybe your class could learn it, and teach it to the whole school . . . Maybe you could tape it and get it played on the radio . . . Maybe kids everywhere could join their voices and sing:

We Say Yes, and We Say Now!

Music and lyrics by Rial Ellsworth, © 1991

We say yes, and we say now— What we need is to help each o - ther.

I say yes, the time is now— For we all need to help our bro - thers.

Come on chil - dren of e - ve - ry na - tion, Clasp your hands a - ro - und the world.

Pledge our - selves to— end— star - va - tion, No more hun - g - ry bo - ys and girls.

I know we can change the world.

4x

38. Invite a speaker from a hunger organization.

Invite someone from a hunger organization to talk to your class or at an assembly. Or maybe some of the parents of your schoolmates have traveled around the world and have seen hunger and could bring in slides. Then again, you might need to let them know about famine and chronic hunger. Perhaps they didn't realize that the people they saw were hungry!

If you invite someone from a local hunger organization, ask him or her to come prepared to let the kids know about hunger near where you live, and how you can help. Ask the person to bring along any video or slides or pictures kids might be interested in.

39. Hold a Hunger Awareness Week at your school.

Suggest to your teacher or principal that you have a Hunger Awareness Week at your school. (You could check the Ending Hunger Calendar on pages 181–183 to get some ideas for a good time to hold it.) During the week, the kids in your class could teach everyone about the two kinds of hunger, about the World Summit and the United Nations Convention on the Rights of the Child, about the importance of giving hungry people chances to end their own hunger, and about how ending hunger helps save the earth. Publicize the week in advance with posters, PA announcements, the school newspaper, flyers, assembly presentations, visits to classrooms —whatever. Include one or more activities such as collecting money for child survival methods like ORS (see page 96) and immunizations; or for a special project that you want your school to fund. Or hold a food drive for the hungry in your area. You could top it off with a fair or special day.

The organizations listed on pages 158–166 have a lot of information and great ideas and activities that could help you organize your week.

Ways to Raise Money

Need some ideas for how to raise money?

Here are fundraising ideas that really work.

Wondering where to send the money you raise?

Look through the description of organizations starting on page 158 to get some ideas. You might want to divide the money up and contribute to several organizations, including one near where you live.

Keep in mind that when you are fundraising it is a great time to talk about ending hunger. Be prepared to tell people what you know!

You will probably need some help in organizing a lot of these activities. No problem! You wanted to get other people involved in ending hunger anyway. This is a great way to get them involved—including parents, teachers, principals, older siblings.

40. Recycle for the end of hunger. Collect cans or bottles for recycling and turn them in for money. Ask your neighbors to let you turn in their cans and bottles as well. For every $10 you send to UNICEF and some of the other organizations, they will be able to buy the vaccine that may very well save a child's life.

Can Our Money Really Make a Difference?

2 cents — Buys a Vitamin A pill. Two pills a year saves a child from blindness. Each year 350,000 kids go blind because they don't have the Vitamin A they need.

13 cents — Immunizes a child against measles. Measles kills 1.5 million children every year.

50 cents — Buys 5 packets of ORS. When mixed with water, ORS can keep a child with diarrhea from dehydrating. Each year 4 million children die from dehydration caused by diarrhea. Two and a half million of them could be saved with ORS.

$1 — Buys antibiotics that can save a child who has pneumonia. Most of the 4 million children who are killed by pneumonia would survive if they were treated with antibiotics.

$1 — Buys enough vaccine to immunize 10 children against polio. Each year 200,000 kids get polio; 20,000 of them die.

41. Hold a "Something-a-thon" for the end of hunger. Almost anyone can do a "Something-a-thon"!

Here's how it works:

- Pick something you like to do—anything. You can walk, bike, dance, bowl, read, swim, hum, play volleyball, keep silent, play—anything you like.

- Let your family and friends and neighbors and teachers and relatives know that you will be, let's say, jogging to raise money for

$10	Covers all the costs of immunizing a child against the four most serious childhood diseases: measles, tetanus, whooping cough, and polio. Immunization would save close to 3 million children's lives a year.
$30	Teaches a mother in Africa how to keep her family healthy over a four-year period.
$45	Helps buy and send a baby scale to South America.
$80	Buys a supply of seeds in Africa that will turn into $400 worth of vegetables after the harvest.
$150	Can provide emergency food to 10 children living in the slums of Asia who are suffering badly from hunger.
$500	Buys and ships a cow to a village.
$500	Pays for a local person to be trained as a health worker. How many lives would be saved? It's hard to measure. Certainly the children of the village and nearby villages. But since the health worker would not only treat the children, but actually teach the parents, who would teach the children, who would teach their children, who would teach their children . . . who knows how many could be saved that way?

the end of hunger. Ask them whether they would be willing to contribute a certain amount of money, like 10 cents or a quarter or a dollar for every mile you jog (or half hour you dance or lap you swim or every 10 minutes you play the violin . . .). Let them know what project or organization will receive the money you raise.

• Write their names down, and the amount they promised to give for every mile (or hour, or 10 minutes) on a list.

- Ask lots of other people whether they would like to support your Something-a-thon as well. Keep track of all the promises.

- Do your activity on one particular day. Really go for it! Think of the difference you're making and the difference the money you're raising is going to make to hungry children. Ask lots of people to support you. Go beyond what you ever thought you could do!

- Afterwards, let all your supporters know how many miles or minutes or laps you completed, and collect their donations.

- When you send in the money you have raised, write a letter telling what you did and why you did it. The people at the organization will be very inspired to learn that the money came from a child, and what you did to earn it.

By the way, if your whole class or school took part in a Something-a-thon, you could raise a **lot** of money. Think about it!

42. **Earn money.** Offer to:

- baby-sit
- mow lawns
- shovel snow
- clean someone's garage or attic
- wash cars
- weed a garden
- exercise pets
- run errands
- read to the elderly
- do yard work
- organize a little kid's birthday party
- help a new mother at home

You might want to reread the "Trick-or-Treating for UNICEF" story on pages 99–106 to review the ideas that Ellen and Sebastian's class came up with.

43. Buy and sell UNICEF cards. See whether your family would like to buy UNICEF cards this Christmas or Hanukkah. The money from the sale of the cards goes to support UNICEF's programs to help kids. (The initials in UNICEF stand for United Nations Children's Emergency Fund.) Or make your presents this year instead of buying them, and with the money saved, make a contribution to UNICEF or one of the other organizations working on child survival.

44. Participate in Oxfam's Fast for a World Harvest. You can join Oxfam's Fast for a World Harvest by deciding not to eat on the Thursday before Thanksgiving. Oxfam (115 Broadway, Boston, MA 02116) will send you a kit and a videotape. Most people who do the fast send in the money they would have spent on food that day, to support Oxfam. You and your friends could get pledges for your fast and really raise some money! Of course, you can do the fast any day you want.

Tell people that you are going to fast on a certain day to raise money to support Oxfam's work in ending hunger, and ask them to pledge a certain amount of money for every hour that you last on your fast. Be sure to let them know why you are doing it and where you will be sending the money.

Set a goal for how long you will try to last. 'Til lunch? 'Til supper? All day? Make sure your parents agree with your goal. As the day goes by you may notice that it is hard to pay attention to anything else when you are hungry. Some teenagers who did this wore special tee shirts on the day they fasted, with the name of every person who was supporting them written on them. That way when they started feeling hungry, they remembered they were not alone.

There are different kinds of fasts. In all of them you should drink plenty of water. You may want to go on a juice fast, which means you eat no solid foods but do drink juices. Or have a fast where you don't eat junk food or snacks for a day—or a whole week. Or you could fast for just one meal or two rather than for the whole day. Be sure your parents agree with whatever plan you come up with. Since you will have a lot of extra time that day (no meals to help prepare, eat, or clean up after), you might want to keep a journal for the day, writing down how it feels and what your thoughts are as the day goes by.

Afterwards, don't forget to collect the money from all the people who said they would support you.

45. Hold a fundraising event. A lot of schools are good at this already. See whether your fellow students and your teachers will hold a fundraising event for ending hunger.

With your school or club or group, hold a bake sale, crafts sale, spaghetti supper, car wash, dance, concert, talent show, or flea market for the end of hunger, and donate the money you raise to whichever organizations you would like to support.

If you do a flea market or garage sale, you could mark every price tag to show what a hunger organization could do with that amount of money. Example: A $1 price tag might read "Buys enough vaccine to immunize 8 children against measles."

46. Clown Around for Kids. Bring Save the Children's Clown Around for Kids campaign to your school. Save the Children will supply batches of red clown noses, for free, to kids in schools. Then, for one week, the kids all sell noses to each other and to the teachers and your parents or

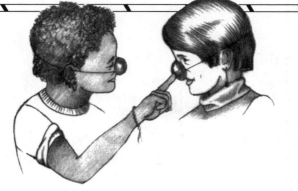

neighbors for $1 or $2 each. At the same time, kids learn about Save the Children's health, nutrition, and education projects for hungry communities around the world. Then everyone comes together for a big celebration, wearing their clown noses. Save the Children (54 Wilton Road, Westport, CT 06880) will send you a booklet on how to organize the campaign and how to make it successful.

47. Organize a World Map-a-thon.
Join Save the Children's newest project for kids to raise money to help other kids: the World Map-a-thon.

It works like the other "thons"—but this time you promise to learn about world geography! Save the Children has a whole kit, complete with maps and certificates and information for your teacher. The kids' job is to learn the location of as many countries as possible during two weeks, and to collect pledges from parents and friends and relatives, based on the number of countries correctly identified.

48. Hold a CROP Walk.

Church World Service, the hunger-fighting agency of the National Council of Churches, can help you organize a CROP Walk. This is an event you can do with people of all ages in your community. Basically, everyone who is going to do the 10-mile walk (or any part of it) asks for sponsors for each mile he or she walks. The money is sent to Church World Service, which uses it for its educational and relief activities and for supporting hungry people in growing their own food. A CROP Walk is great fun when people of all ages join in: babies in strollers, roller skaters, housewives, kindergartners, old people, high school kids, kids like you. In some places CROP Walks raise thousands of dollars. Check it out!

Fundraising tip:

Want to double or triple your results? Talk to a grown-up about "matching funds." Perhaps the PTA or a Rotary, Kiwanis, Jaycees, or Lions club or a restaurant or store in your town would be willing to match funds that the kids in your school raise from any of the activities we've listed so far.

Matching funds means that the adults agree to donate the same amount of money that the kids raise—and sometimes even twice or three times the amount you raise! It's a great way to **multiply** your results! The grown-ups will probably be so inspired by what you're doing that they will be delighted to match your funds. Just ask!

49. Hold a community cleanup for the end of hunger.

The National Student Campaign Against Hunger and Homelessness organizes a hunger cleanup every April. It's the biggest student community service event in the United States. The cleanup is set up for high school- and college-age kids, but see how it works. Maybe you could organize your own version for the kids in your school.

- Come up with a list of things that need doing in your community, like picking up trash, weeding public areas, cleaning up a beachfront. Maybe someone from the mayor's office could give you some ideas.

- Pick a day for your community cleanup.

- Have the kids in your class get their parents, relatives, and neighbors to sponsor them for the three hours they'll spend cleaning up your community. That means, the adults promise to donate a certain amount of money for the three hours the kids will be working.

- On the day of the cleanup, the kids do the work. Parents are of course useful in helping to get rid of trash, weeds, make trips to the dump, and so on.

- Then you go back to the people who promised to donate, you collect the money, and you add it all together to see how much your cleanup raised. Send it to the organizations you want to support.

- This project takes a little work to organize. You might want to suggest it to the PTA or the Scouts or some other club that's looking for a way to get involved in ending hunger.

50. Just ask for it! Another way
to raise money is just to ask for it! When you let people know what you know—that millions of children suffer and die from hunger, and that what is needed is to give hungry people a chance to end their own hunger, and that the world leaders have promised to take action—and when you let them know that you're collecting money to help end the problem, they will probably really thank you for giving them a chance to contribute. Try it and see!

And Keep in Mind...

Track down and help end hunger near where you live. Hunger is not limited to one country or one region of the world. When you're raising money and talking about the World Summit for Children and the difference between famine and chronic hunger, keep in mind the hungry in your own country. Find out who is hungry in your area, and what is being done about it. Look into feeding programs, but also investigate what laws need to be passed to end hunger locally, and which politicians are working on the problem. The United States House of Representatives has a special Select Committee on Hunger, which will send a *Hunger Report* bulletin to anyone who asks for it. They can give you information on how to make your community hunger-free (House Select Committee on Hunger, 505 Ford Office Building, Washington, DC 20515).

Ending hunger is for anyone and everyone.
Truthfully, we can each do the things we like best or are best at—and contribute **that** to the end of hunger.

For example, if you are a writer, write about the end of hunger; if you are a singer, sing about it; if you are a storyteller, tell stories about it; if you are a runner, run for it; if you are an artist, draw about it; if you are a scientist, study it; if you are a balloon-blower-upper, blow up balloons for it; if you are an actor, put on plays about it ... We're all good at something, and that means we each have our own special contribution to make to ending hunger.

Kids Ending Hunger– What Does It Really Matter?

What's So Good About Ending Hunger?

Did you ever walk around feeling sad all day, but you couldn't quite remember what you were sad about? Then, when you remembered what the sad thing was, you got extra sad? Then you forgot about it for a while, but the sadness stayed in your heart?

It's a little like that with hunger in our world.

Sometimes we think about it. We read a book like this one, we see some pictures of hungry people on TV or in the newspaper. And we take whatever actions we can think of.

But the sadness of a world in which so many thousands of kids die and are crippled and harmed by hunger is a sadness that each of us lives with, whether or not we are thinking about it. It surrounds us. It is a silent pain in the heart of all humanity.

So we are inviting you to become a hero—no kidding—and to free the world from this terrible sorrow.

But that's not all.

There is something great to think about.

Think of it this way:

Imagine a world without hunger . . .

Imagine a world where families—all families—can take care of themselves . . .

Imagine a world where children—all children—grow strong, go to school, and can offer the world their own particular joys and talents . . .

Imagine the sadness removed from the faces of parents who cannot feed their children, and the joy in the faces and bodies of healthy, happy children all across our earth . . .

Imagine your own heart knowing that people on our planet go to bed with food in their bellies each night, that the right to eat is one of the rights of being a human being.

Plus—imagine the enormous contribution to the world that those millions of well-fed human beings will make!

Can you imagine it?

Can you imagine the great happiness, the great celebration of the human family, when we have freed our world from hunger?

A dream? Yes, of course it is.

But is it possible? Could it really happen?

You bet.

Want to be one of the ones who make the dream come true?

So . . .

Ending hunger is possible. It will take money. And it will take commitment.

We get committed when we really, really, really want something to happen.

That's where kids like you—and your friends, and classmates, and neighbors, and family—come in.

By doing some of the activities and projects in this book,

by coming up with some of your own ideas,

by taking the hungry children into your heart,

by finding out more about hunger yourself,

by sharing the information with others,

by asking people to get involved, to commit themselves to ending hunger, you will be taking actions that will allow our human family to see that ending hunger is everybody's job, actions that will bring about the end of hunger on our planet.

You. Yes, you!

If you get into action—and enough others around the world do as well —we **can** end hunger on our planet.

The question is: will we do it?

Resources— How Can I Find Out More?

Groups Working to End World Hunger

These are some of the many, many organizations in the United States and in other countries working on ending world hunger. These are only a few of the many organizations springing up all the time as people become aware of and take on ending hunger. Many of them have excellent written materials to send you. They also have videotapes, films, and filmstrips, which they lend for free or for a small fee.

Any and all of them would appreciate receiving your contributions.

You'll notice that this list might make it seem that most of the work to end hunger is being done by people in the United States. But it isn't. Most of the work to end world hunger is being done by the hungry people themselves! The groups listed here are helping the hungry people end their own hunger.

Africare
440 R St. NW
Washington, DC 20001
(202) 462-3614

Africare works to make life better for people in 22 countries of Africa. Ten dollars provides 100 pounds of fertilizer for crops, feeds two people for a month, or provides seed to plant a field.

American Jewish World Service
1290 Avenue of the Americas, 11th floor
New York, NY 10104
(212) 468-7380

The American Jewish World Service provides emergency relief and development assistance to people of all religions in Africa, Asia, and Latin America. They particularly focus on helping with health and agricultural projects.

Bread for the World
802 Rhode Island Ave. NE
Washington, DC 20018
(202) 722-4100/(202) 269-0200

Volunteers from Bread for the World urge politicians in the United States to vote for policies that will help end hunger. The group gives advice on how to begin a letter-writing campaign to members of Congress.

CARE
660 First Ave.
New York, NY 10016
(212) 686-3110

Health workers, teachers, and farming experts are sent by CARE to help hungry and poor people learn how to take care of themselves and their families. They do lots with child survival activities. Donations are spent on things like wells, seeds, medicine, and equipment. They have great materials for kids and educators.

Catholic Relief Services
209 W. Fayette St.
Baltimore, MD 21201
(410) 625-2220

Catholic Relief Services works in over 70 countries, distributing food, clothing, and medicine in times of disaster, and also helps local groups provide opportunities to the hungry in those countries.

Childreach
155 Plan Way
Warwick, RI 02886-1099
1-800-556-7918

Formerly called Foster Parents Plan, this group has been improving the lives of children and their families since 1937. Its focus is on child survival activities, and on matching children with families who want to help them.

Children's Aid International
PO Box 480155
Los Angeles, CA 90048
(213) 936-8917

Children's Aid International provides medical care, improved nutrition, education, and opportunities to children and their families. Sponsorship helps improve conditions for the entire family and provides money in an emergency fund to be used in case of a disaster.

Children's Defense Fund

122 C St. NW
Washington, DC 20001
(202) 628-8787

The Children's Defense Fund concentrates on gathering information about what is happening with children in the United States of America. They watch out for how the programs and policies affecting children are carried out.

Christian Children's Fund Inc.

Richmond, VA 23261 (That's right—they have no street address!)
(804) 644-4654

Christian Children's Fund Inc. provides sponsorship to help children in the developing world. Sponsors and children get to know each other through letters.

Church World Service

475 Riverside Dr.
New York, NY 10115
(212) 870-2257

Church World Service provides food and blankets and tools in times of emergency. They teach villagers about eating properly, reading and writing, and how to get better jobs. The group also sponsors a CROP Walk each year for people who are willing to walk 10 kilometers to raise money.

End Hunger Network

222 N. Beverly Dr.
Beverly Hills, CA 90210
(213) 273-3179

The End Hunger Network gets the media (TV, movie stars, newspapers) to speak the message of the poor and hungry to as many people as possible, so that ending hunger becomes a national priority.

Food Research and Action Center
1875 Connecticut Ave. NW, Suite 540
Washington, DC 20009
(202) 986-2200

The Center studies hunger in the United States and helps coordinate hunger groups, religious organizations, legal groups, and people interested in ending hunger locally.

Heifer Project International
PO Box 808
Little Rock, AR 72203
(501) 376-6836

Heifer Project International sends animals such as cows, goats, pigs, and chickens to poor families so that they can feed themselves and earn money. One dollar buys a chicken or duck; a $10 donation starts a whole flock of ducks or chickens; for $25 you can send a supply of bees; a $150 contribution buys a goat that gives a family eight cups of milk a day.

Helen Keller International
15 W. 16th St.
New York, NY 10011
(212) 807-5800

Helen Keller International, inspired by the famous writer and lecturer who became deaf and blind when she was a baby, encourages governments and private organizations to take care of the blind in their countries and helps teach health care to prevent blindness and other eye diseases caused by hunger. They train health workers to be able to go into the villages to help the people directly.

The Hunger Project
1 Madison Ave.
New York, NY 10010
(212) 532-4255

This international organization is creating a worldwide movement to end hunger by giving millions of people around the world the facts about hunger and asking them to get involved. In addition to working with leaders of countries to figure out how they can end hunger, the Hunger Project encourages people to support the many groups and organizations that are working to end hunger by the year 2000. The group sponsors Youth Ending Hunger groups all around the world.

IDEX
827 Valencia St.
San Francisco, CA 94110
(415) 824-8384

IDEX (International Development Exchange) connects hungry people who want to start projects to end their own hunger with groups or people in the United States who want to help them. All the projects that IDEX sets up are run by the people in those countries. A school program provides lots of information to the students who are supporting their projects.

Institute for Food and Development Policy
145 Ninth St.
San Francisco, CA 94103
(415) 864-8555

This research and education center puts out information on the causes of hunger and food problems in the United States and around the world. The Institute is eager to provide information, educate, and get everyone involved so that hunger can be ended.

InterAction
1717 Massachusetts Ave. NW, 8th floor
Washington, DC 20036
(202) 667-8227

A special organization in the United States, InterAction is a collection of lots of the organizations working on ending hunger. If you want to know about all the organizations, including which ones are doing what kinds of projects, you could write to InterAction.

International Eye Foundation
7801 Norfolk Ave.
Bethesda, MD 20814
(301) 986-1830

The International Eye Foundation provides Vitamin A pills to the kids who need them and teaches the villagers which foods have Vitamin A in them. The group also helps them grow those foods.

Lasting Links

6231 Leesburg Pike, Suite 612
Falls Church, VA 22024
(703) 241-3700

Lasting Links is a clearinghouse for small-scale projects from many organizations. They will match up schools or other groups with relief or development projects to suit the groups' interests.

Oxfam America

115 Broadway
Boston, MA 02116
(617) 482-1211

This group has many projects to help villagers help themselves and provides emergency help when needed. They also put out educational materials to make people aware of hunger. On the Thursday before Thanksgiving, Oxfam sponsors a fast and invites everyone to donate the money they would have spent on food.

Partners of the Americas

1424 K St. NW, Suite 700
Washington, DC 20005
(202) 628-3300

Partners of the Americas matches each state in the United States with a place in Latin America or the Caribbean that needs some help. They educate the people, helping them improve their lives and earn money. You can find out where the "partner" is for your state, and how you can help the people living there.

Project Concern

3550 Afton Road
San Diego, CA 92123
(619) 279-9690

Project Concern works to provide low-cost health care and health education, including the Child Survival Campaign. They focus on helping pregnant women take care of themselves and their babies, and on teaching villagers and other hungry people about food and how to keep from becoming sick. Thousands of schoolchildren take part in their Walk for Mankind each year as a way to raise money to support "Health Care for All."

RESULTS
236 Massachusetts Ave. NE, Suite 300
Washington, DC 20002-4980
(202) 543-9340

RESULTS volunteers write to politicians in the United States and ask them to vote for laws that will start to eliminate hunger. There are RESULTS volunteer groups all over the United States who write their elected officials, call them, and even visit them to ask them to make ending hunger their priority. They also work with the media. Their newsletter, *Entry Point*, reports on current political issues that affect ending hunger and what actions individuals can take on those issues

Save the Children
54 Wilton Road
Westport, CT 06880
(203) 697-0264/(203) 226-7271

Save the Children helps children who are poor to have a better life, with programs to immunize kids, to teach them how to read, and to make sure they're eating and growing properly. Their programs are in many countries around the world, including the United States. They have a number of programs for kids who want to help, including their School-to-School program, Clown Around for Kids, and the World Map-a-thon. Their booklet "Ten Ways to Get to Five" explains the Child Survival Campaign.

Seva Foundation
8 N. San Pedro Road
San Rafael, CA 94903
(415) 492-1829

Seva is an international service organization begun by people who worked with the campaign to eliminate smallpox. It is dedicated to relieving suffering, while helping people become self-sufficient.

Donations are used to help end blindness in Nepal, to support GOBI programs, and to help with other projects around the world.

Trickle Up Program
54 Riverside Dr., PHE
New York, NY 10024
(212) 362-7958

The Trickle Up Program assists hungry people in setting up self-help projects to end their hunger, by helping them start or expand small businesses that will provide them money to buy food and other necessities.

United Nations Development Programme
1 UN Plaza
New York, NY 10017
(212) 906-5302

This is one of several branches of the United Nations focused on improving the living conditions of people around the globe. The UNDP has offices in 112 countries. They try to make a permanent difference in the self-reliance of people in developing countries.

U.S. Committee for UNICEF
333 E. 38th St.
New York, NY 10016
(212) 686-5522

UNICEF saves and improves the lives of children in more than 100 countries by helping people living in villages get good health care, education, clean water, and emergency help when they need it. UNICEF is also very involved with the Child Survival Campaign. Kids often support UNICEF by collecting money while trick-or-treating on Halloween.

World Hunger Education Service
PO Box 29056
Washington, DC 20017
(202) 298-9503

The World Hunger Education Service studies United States food policy, third-world development, and economic justice issues.

World Hunger Year

261 W. 35th St., #1402
New York, NY 10001-1906
(212) 629-8850

World Hunger Year is a nonprofit organization devoted to the idea that every year is "world hunger year" until hunger is ended. It informs the public, the media, and the policymakers about the extent and causes of hunger in the United States and abroad, and also starts and organizes actions to fight hunger, poverty, and homelessness.

World Share

3350 E St.
San Diego, CA 92102
(619) 525-2200

These workers help thousands of families in the U.S., Mexico, and Guatemala by teaching them how to work together to feed themselves and how to be able to buy more food by buying it as a group.

World Vision

919 W. Huntington Dr.
Monrovia, CA 91016
(818) 357-7979

World Vision is a Christian organization that provides emergency relief and works to give hungry people opportunities in over 90 countries. It helps more than 800,000 children each year.

Resources for Teachers

Note: Many of the organizations in the previous section have excellent materials designed for the classroom as well.

Africa Education Module (1990)
The Hunger Project
1388 Sutter St.
San Francisco, CA 94109

Child Survival—What Can I Do? (1987)
The End Hunger Network
222 N. Beverly Dr.
Beverly Hills, CA 90210

Children Hungering for Justice (1991)
Office on Global Education
Church World Service
2115 N. Charles St.
Baltimore, MD 21218

Educators Care Package and
Partners in Child Survival: Educational Activities
CARE
660 First Ave.
New York, NY 10016

Ending Hunger: It's Possible, It's Happening (1979) by Jerold Ciekot
and Douglas Gwyn
American Friends Service Committee
1501 Cherry St.
Philadelphia, PA 19102

Exploding the Hunger Myths: A High School Curriculum (1987) by
Sonja Williams
Institute for Food and Development Policy
145 Ninth St.
San Francisco, CA 94103

Famine and Chronic Persistent Hunger: A Life and Death Distinction
(1989) Video and Teacher's Guide
The Hunger Project
1388 Sutter St.
San Francisco, CA 94109

*Feed, Need, Greed: Food, Resources, and Population—A High School
Curriculum* (1981)
Science for the People
897 Main St.
Cambridge, MA 02139

First Food Curriculum (1984) by Laurie Rubin
Institute for Food and Development Policy
145 Ninth St.
San Francisco, CA 94103

Food for All—Teaching Against Hunger (1982)
Global Perspectives in Education
The American Forum for Global Education
45 John St., Suite 1200
New York, NY 10038

Global Primer: Skills for a Changing World (1986) by H. Thomas
Collins and Fred Czarra
Center for Teaching International Relations
University of Denver
Denver, CO 80208

*Have You Ever Been Hungry? A Church School Curriculum Guide for
Grades 3–4, 5–6, 7–8* by Patricia L. Kutzner and Linda Stoerkel
United Church Board for Moeland Ministries
Division of Publications
132 W. 31st St.
New York, NY 10001

Healthy Children/Healthy World (1986) by Cynthia Dean, R.N., M.P.H.
U.S. Committee for UNICEF
333 E. 38th St.
New York, NY 10016

Hunger Action Handbook (1987), Leslie Withers and Tom Peterson, editors
Seeds Magazine
222 E. Lake Dr.
Decatur, GA 30030

Keeping the Promise (1991)
RESULTS
236 Massachusetts Ave. NE, Suite 300
Washington, DC 20002-4980

Knowing, Caring, Sharing: Children, Hunger, and Poverty (1989)
Heifer Project International
PO Box 808
Little Rock, AR 72203

See Me, Share My World (1989)
Childreach
155 Plan Way
Warwick, RI 02886-1099

Teaching About Food and Hunger: 33 Activities (1977) by George Otero and Gary Smith
Center for Teaching International Relations
University of Denver
Denver, CO 80208

World Food Day Curriculum
Church World Service Office on Global Education
2115 N. Charles St.
Baltimore, MD 21128

World Food Day Packet
National Committee for World Food Day
1001 22nd St. NW, Suite 300
Washington, DC 20437

World Hunger: Learning to Face the Challenge by Carrol Joy and Patrick Regan
(no longer in print, but worth searching the library for)

Audiovisual Materials

Almost all the hunger organizations have videos, slides, or films that they make available for little or no charge.

Always preview the material before you show it to a group to see whether it will work for the ages and interests of your group.

Here are some of the places you can contact to borrow audiovisual materials about ending hunger. Listed are a few, but not all, of the materials they have.

American Friends Service Committee, 1501 Cherry St., Philadelphia, PA 19102.

Hamburger USA (28-minute slide show about the role of the humble hamburger)

Church World Service

Charlie Cheddar's Choice (13-minute filmstrip introducing the basic facts of hunger and some solutions, through the story of a middle-class mouse named Charlie)

Children of Sun/Children of Rain (filmstrip about the difference between the lives of the rich and the poor children of Latin America)

Hunger Hotline Revisited (16-minute filmstrip about the causes of hunger)

More (3-minute cartoon showing what can happen to a people when they want more, more, more)

Remember Me (17-minute film. True story about what the lives of poor children are like.)

Spaceship Earth (15-minute film made by elementary school children that looks at some of the world's problems, including hunger and overpopulation)

The Hunger Project

Famine and Chronic Persistent Hunger: A Life and Death Distinction (11-minute video about the important difference between famine and chronic persistent hunger)

Journey Films

With Oscar in Peru (11-minute video about the life of a boy in a rural Peruvian village, and the choices that his family and village must make)

Oxfam America

Harvest of Hunger (20-minute video showing that hunger is not caused by too many people and not enough food)

U.S. Committee for UNICEF

341 (13-minute video shows both the extent of the problem of hunger, and how available and affordable the solutions are; the title refers to the number of children who die of hunger and disease during its running time)

Especially the Children (18-minute film, narrated by Liv Ullmann, about the need for food and emergency services)

Books About Hunger for Parents and Educators

The following is a brief list of books on the subject of ending hunger that may be useful for parents or educators who want to become better informed.

Children and Development in the 1990s: A UNICEF Sourcebook
UNICEF, 1990

A comprehensive discussion "meant for all those who wish to extend their knowledge of any of the themes under discussion at, or around, the (World) Summit (for Children), stating the issues and providing readers with the background information, explanations, definitions, data, and references they may require to obtain a deeper understanding of the subjects."

Ending Hunger: An Idea Whose Time Has Come
The Hunger Project (illustrated)
New York: Praeger, 1985

A sourcebook with an overview of basic facts about world hunger, including statistics, graphs, charts, and many photographs.

Facts for Life
New York: UNICEF, DIPA 1990

Simple explanation with powerful photographs of what is needed to improve the health of children in the developing world. Created and published in partnership with many of the world's leading medical and children's organizations. Could be used with children.

Food First: Beyond the Myth of Scarcity
Frances Moore Lappé and Joseph Collins
New York: Ballantine Books, 1982, revised

Study on population growth, the Green Revolution, U.S. foreign aid, the World Bank, and agribusiness.

How the Other Half Dies: The Real Reasons for World Hunger
Susan George
Montclair, N.J.: Allanheld, Osmun & Co., 1977

A well-researched study of the link between hunger and the distribution of resources among both industrialized and poor countries.

Human Development Report, 1990–1991
United Nations Development Programme (UNDP)
New York (annual)

A report produced by UNDP that addresses the human dimension of development. It includes a comprehensive set of human development indicators.

Hunger 1990: A Report on the State of World Hunger
Washington, DC: Bread for the World (annual)

A report on the state of world hunger that includes regional updates and information on successful ideas for ending hunger.

Ill Fares the Land: Essays on Food, Hunger, and Power
Susan George
New York: Viking Penguin, 1990

A comprehensive assessment of the connection between environmental and development issues, with recommendations for policy actions.

Our Common Future
Oxford, N.Y.: World Commission on Environment and Development, 1987

   The World Commission on Environment and Development was asked by the United Nations to formulate a "global agenda for change." This book is the commission's historic report.

Physician Task Force on Hunger in America: The Growing Epidemic
Middletown, Conn.: Wesleyan University Press, 1985

   Well-documented report on the extent of hunger in the United States. Contains many personal stories.

Population Data Sheet
Population Reference Bureau
Washington, D.C. (annual)

   A concise poster-sized sheet displaying at a glance the critical indicators for every country and region on earth.

The State of the World's Children: U.S. Committee for UNICEF
(annual)
James P. Grant
New York: Oxford University Press, 1990

   Provides statistics, research, discussion, and case studies about efforts to increase child survival rates around the world.

Ten Steps to Five
Westport, Conn.: Save the Children

   Very simple and straightforward display of the elements of the Child Survival Campaign.

World Food, Population, and Development
Gigi M. Berardi, editor
Totowa, N.J.: Rowman and Allanheld, 1985

   A collection of readings in the interrelated areas of food, population, and development.

World Hunger: Twelve Myths
Frances Moore Lappé and Joseph Collins
New York: Grove Press, 1986

Presents myths about how hunger is generated and explains how people throughout the world are trying to achieve food self-sufficiency.

Books for Kids

Here are some books that may be of interest to you. Some of them give you a picture of what life is like for kids who are suffering from hunger or who live in places where there are many hungry kids. Others are included because they tell the story of courageous kids who want to make something happen, want to make the world a better place.

Most of the books here are fiction. Your school and local librarian will be able to show you a lot of others on these topics.

If you are interested in learning more about what life is like in countries around the world (nonfiction), check out the 914–919 section in your library.

A friendly librarian can be an enormous help to you in finding out more about hunger, kids, life in other lands, and making a difference in the world. Check it out!

The number in parentheses suggests the reading grade level.

Fiction

Ballard, John. *Monsoon* (6–9), 1985, 240 pages.

A teenage girl goes with her family to India, where she and her friends have a series of exciting adventures.

Bergman, Tamar. *The Boy from Over There* (5–9), 1988, 180 pages.

A boy whose family is lost in World War II is taken to Israel to live on a kibbutz with an uncle. He refuses to talk or play with anyone, and the other children have a hard time accepting him.

When war comes to Israel, the children's courage and cooperation are tested in life-and-death situations.

Branson, Karen. *The Potato Eaters* (5–8), 1979, 160 pages.

Faced with hunger and illness in the 1846 potato famine in Ireland, the O'Connor family make the difficult decision to leave their home and emigrate to America. The novel tells the story of the family's strength in the face of all they must do to stay alive.

Burton, Hester. *In Spite of All Terror* (7–9), 1968, 203 pages.

A 15-year-old orphan from the slums of London is sent away during the bombing of World War II to the countryside, where her courage is needed to save the lives of English soldiers under enemy fire.

Cameron, Ann. *The Most Beautiful Place in the World* (3–7), 1988, 57 pages.

A little boy in the mountains of Guatemala must live without his mother and father. He has a hard life trying to earn money to stay alive. His grandmother helps him find a way to be able to go to school.

Dixon, Paige. *Promises to Keep* (6–8), 1974, 165 pages.

A boy in a small New Hampshire town is horrified when a distant cousin who is half Vietnamese and half American comes to stay. While the visit causes problems for everyone, Charles and the whole town are deeply changed by the hate—and the friendship—that are shown.

Fenton, Edward. *The Refugee Summer* (6–9), 1982, 262 pages.

Five children visiting Greece want to have an adventure that will transform their lives. The adventure becomes real when thousands of refugees flood into Greece, and their suffering stirs the children into action.

Forman, James. *Follow the River* (8–adult), 1975, 185 pages.

Paul and Jananki go to India to take part in a friendship march that is to match the one Gandhi took 15 years earlier. They find themselves in danger when their beliefs are tested and their lives threatened.

Garrigue, Sheila. *All the Children Were Sent Away* (5–8), 1976, 171 pages.

Eight-year-old Sara has to leave London when the bombing starts and her parents stay behind to fight the Nazis. Her adventures on the long sea voyage to Canada include being torpedoed by a German submarine.

Harris, Mark Jonathan. *Come the Morning* (5–9), 1989, 169 pages.

Ben and his younger brother and sister go with their mom to Los Angeles to look for his father, where they become homeless. The novel gives a believable picture of what life is like for children who become homeless in the United States. The family's courage and love in the face of the situation are inspiring.

Ho, Mingfong. *Sing to the Dawn* (5–8), 1975, 160 pages.

When she wins the scholarship competition, a girl in Thailand faces the anger and hostility of her father and brother, who feel that further schooling is wasted on a girl. The frustrations, hardships, and injustices of everyday life in a village in Southeast Asia are shown.

Holman, Felice. *Secret City, U.S.A.* (6–9), 1990, 199 pages.

Two 13-year-old street boys get the idea of turning a broken-down section of the city into a safe place for homeless kids and families. In spite of danger and opposition, they discover what hope, will, and imagination can make happen.

Holman, Felice. *The Wild Children* (6–9), 1983, 150 pages.

A band of homeless children in Russia escape and survive through their bravery and friendships.

Howard, Moses L. *The Ostrich Chase* (5–8), 1974, 118 pages.

A young African girl living in the Kalahari desert secretly practices using a bow and arrow so she can hunt like the boys and men. She accidentally wounds her grandmother, and they are forced to travel alone through dangerous country to the water hole.

Kidd, Diana. *Onion Tears* (4–6), 1989, 62 pages.

A little Vietnamese girl who has lost her family and has seen the pain of war slowly learns to trust again in her new home in a new country.

Naidoo, Beverley. *Chain of Fire* (7–9), 1989, 245 pages.

Fifteen-year-old Naledi and her friends are being forced by the South African government to leave their village and move to a barren land. The kids refuse. What happens to them and their village in the face of apartheid causes them to become a "chain of fire." (The author, who grew up in South Africa, writes about her book: "I believe we owe it to young people here to help them understand what the struggle against an evil system is about. How can we hope for peace if we deny our children access to that knowledge?")

Naidoo, Beverley. *Journey to Jo'burg* (4–7), 1985, 80 pages.

A 13-year-old girl and her little brother travel 300 miles by themselves to find their mother so she can come home and save their very sick baby sister.

Sacks, Margaret. *Beyond Safe Boundaries* (7–9), 1989, 156 pages.

A 13-year-old white South African girl finds out what is really going on in her country when her older sister goes away to college and gets involved with the anti-government movement, which is opposed to apartheid.

Wartski, Maureen. *A Long Way Home* (6–9), 1980, 155 pages.

An orphaned Vietnamese boy is sent to America to live and finds trouble among children who don't accept him.

Yolen, Jane. *Children of the Wolf* (6–9), 1984, 136 pages.

Although fiction, this story is based on a real story of two children in India who were raised by wolves. In this story, a 14-year-old boy in a Christian orphanage in India tries to teach the wild children words and human habits, and to protect them from the other children in the orphanage.

Nonfiction

Ashabranner, Brent. *Children of the Maya* (7–9), 1986, 90 pages.

The true story of Guatemalan Mayan Indians who fled from their mountain villages out of fear for their lives. This book tells the story of a group of them who settled in Florida, and of the many changes in lifestyle they faced in coming to such a very different land. Pictures.

Ashabranner, Brent and Melissa. *Into a Strange Land: Unaccompanied Refugee Youth in America* (6–adult), 1982, 118 pages.

In words and pictures, tells the story of children who have been sent to America to begin new lives, and about the people who are helping them.

Frank, Anne. *The Diary of a Young Girl* (7–9), 1967, 312 pages.

The famous diary of a 13-year-old Jewish Dutch girl whose family was forced into hiding by the Nazis during World War II.

Goldfarb, Mace, MD. *Fighters, Refugees, Immigrants* (4–8), 1982, 39 pages.

With many color photographs, a doctor shows what it was like to help Laotian families who were forced to flee for their lives to a refugee camp in Thailand.

Klyce, Katherine Perrow, and Virginia Overton McLean. *Kenya, Jambo* (3–8), 1989, 34 pages.

In pictures and children's art, an introduction to the African country of Kenya. With drawings, many done by kids, the history, people, culture, language, and wildlife of Kenya are shown.

Leinwand, Gerald. *Hunger and Malnutrition in America* (7–adult), 1985, 90 pages.

Talks about hunger in America and what can be done to end it.

Loescher, Gil, and Ann Dull Loescher. *The World's Refugees: A Test of Humanity* (6–adult), 1982, 145 pages.

In words and pictures, tells the stories of the millions of children and adults who have had to leave their homes and countries. The book addresses where the refugees come from, where they go, how they get there, and what happens when they arrive.

Books of Photographs of Kids and People Around the World

Children of Many Lands, by Hanns Reich, 1958, 125 pages of photographs (black and white)

The Family of Man, created by Edward Steichen for the Museum of Modern Art, 1955, 210 pages of photographs (black and white)

One World, One People: A Collection of Photographs and Essays on the Power of the Human Experience, photographs by Yoshiaki Nagashima, words by Robert White and Koichi Shimazu, 1984, 98 pages of photographs and short essays (color)

Magazines and Newsletters

Children's Express
245 Seventh Ave., 5th floor
New York, NY 10001-7302

A bimonthly national newsletter produced by teenagers.

First Call for Children
UNICEF
3 UN Plaza
New York, NY 10017

A new, bimonthly UNICEF publication (adult reading level).

Hunger Notes
World Hunger Education Service
PO Box 29056
Washington, DC 20017

A journal of the World Hunger Education Service, *Hunger Notes* is an information exchange on world hunger, domestic hunger, and economic development.

Population Data Sheet
Population Reference Bureau
777 14th St. NW, Suite 800
Washington, DC 20005

The Population Data Sheet is a poster, not a magazine, that is published every year. It has more information on it than probably any other single piece of paper you will ever see, including what countries have ended hunger that year! For example, the 1990 Population Data Sheet showed the seven countries that ended hunger that year. It's practically an encyclopedia in itself! It costs about $1.25 and contains all sorts of facts about each country and region of the world: things like the infant mortality rates, the birth rates, population, death rates and a lot more.

Seeds: Christians Concerned About Hunger
PO Box 6170
Waco, TX 76706

A magazine with articles about local and global hunger and what is being done to solve it. Adult level.

Why Magazine
World Hunger Year
261 W. 35th St., #1402
New York, NY 10001-1906

A publication of the nonprofit organization World Hunger Year (WHY).

Your World
7219 Blair Road NW
Washington, DC 20012

An international newspaper for young people, designed to increase awareness of other countries and other cultures.

Youth News Service Newsletter
2025 Pennsylvania Ave. NW, Suite 501
Washington, DC 20006

A twice-monthly newsletter about youth-related issues. For kids.

Calendar of Ending-Hunger Activities

Here are some activities that you, your family, or your school may want to participate in. You can mark them in big letters on your family or school calendar.

Valentine Vision—February 14

On or near February 14, classes talk about hunger in the world, and hold a "Moment of Vision." Everyone is silent for 60 seconds; during that moment, students are asked to imagine a world where all children have enough to eat. Students are invited to make valentines, which are sent and distributed to children in other countries.

Contact Valentine Vision, 78 Summer St., Weston, MA 02193, (617) 894-1166, for their materials.

World Health Day—April 7

World Health Day was established by the World Health Organization in 1948. Write to the American Association of World Health, 2001 S St. NW, #530, Washington, DC 20009, for suggestions and ideas for what you can do.

Hunger Cleanup—April 16

The National Student Campaign Against Hunger Cleanup involves older students in many different cities and towns all across the United States.

On Hunger Cleanup Day, April 16, thousands of students volunteer three hours of their time to help out in a community service project in their area. The students get sponsors—people who will give money to a hunger organization for each hour that the students work. The National Student Campaign also participates in many World Food Day (October 16) activities, and can provide ideas.

Contact: National Student Campaign Against Hunger, 29 Temple Place, Boston, MA 02111.

Save the Children Day—May 1

Save the Children has a number of programs designed for kids to participate in, including:

School-to-School Partnership Program

School presentations

Sponsoring a child

Clown Around for Kids

Youth Congress

World Map-a-thon

Child Survival Campaign activities

May 1, Save the Children Day, would be a good time to take part in any or all of them!

Contact: Save the Children, 54 Wilton Road, Westport, CT 06880.

World Food Day—October 16

All around the world on October 16, individuals and groups focus their attention on the problems of hunger and food. The National Committee for World Food Day puts out some great materials for classroom activities, and ways to involve your whole town or community.

Contact: U.S. National Committee for World Food Day, 1001 22nd St. NW, Suite 300, Washington, DC 20437, for help in planning your activities.

Trick-or-Treat for UNICEF—Halloween, October 31

A favorite way that kids all across the U.S. can and do help other kids stay alive and stay healthy is by raising money for UNICEF.

You may want to team up with whoever is organizing the UNICEF drive in your school (maybe the PTA), or you could get in touch with UNICEF yourself. Then again, how about if you take charge of the whole drive this year, instead of the adults!

You could make it a real contest this year, with all the grades competing: can cute little fairy princesses in the second grade raise more money than pirates in the fifth? You could ask some stores to donate some great prizes for the winners.

The whole project will probably be much more meaningful for everyone if you've let the kids know in advance some of the facts about hunger, and the miracles the money they collect will create in the lives of kids suffering from hunger. Even kids who think they're too old to go out and trick-or-treat for candy could go out to collect for UNICEF this year.

For information and collection boxes, contact: U.S. Committee for UNICEF, 333 E. 38th St., New York, NY 10016, (212) 686-5522.

Oxfam's Fast for a World Harvest—Thursday before Thanksgiving

On the Thursday before Thanksgiving, many people fast for one meal or for the entire day and donate the money they would have spent on food that day to Oxfam America, an organization that sponsors programs both in relief (helping out in time of trouble) and development (working with people so that they become self-sufficient).

You can get a "Fast Kit" from Oxfam America for no charge. Contact: Oxfam America, 115 Broadway, Boston, MA 02116.

Thanksgiving and Christmas Seasons

Thanksgiving and Christmas are excellent times of year to talk to people about the world's children, about hunger, and about giving money!

About the
Information in
This Book

When you write about something real that is taking place now, it doesn't stay the same after you write about it.

Situations change, numbers change, organizations move, new things happen.

Please don't be disappointed if you find that some of the information in this book doesn't agree with something you read in the papers in the future or see on TV or hear someone say.

We recommend that you investigate if you find disagreements. What are the statements based on? What facts? What opinions?

Then you may need to decide for yourself what you think about a particular subject.

Another thing:

In *Kids Ending Hunger* we talk about some pretty big numbers: the number of kids who are hungry, the number that are dying. None of the numbers are exact. For one thing, the hungry people are not all standing in line somewhere waiting to be counted, wearing signs that say "I am suffering from hunger." They are living in distant villages and huge cities and it is really hard to get an accurate count. Then, too, if children die of measles, but it was only because their bodies were so weakened by hunger that measles could kill them, do you count those as hunger deaths?

Scientists and experts have done their best to figure out the numbers.

We may never find out the exact numbers.

But whatever they are, we can all agree that they are way, way, way too big.

Specific References

Almost 1 billion people are hungry.
- The United Nations Development Programme estimates 800 million.
- The World Food Council estimates 550 million.
- The Hunger Project estimates between 500 million and 1 billion.
- The World Bank says that more than 1 billion people are living in a state of absolute poverty.

Each day 40,000 children die of largely preventable hunger and disease.
   —UNICEF State of the World's Children report, 1990

More people have died of hunger in the last 5 years than in all the wars in the last 150 years.
   —The Hunger Project, *A Shift in the Wind #5*

The cost of ORS, immunizations, Vitamin A, and so on.
   —UNICEF State of the World's Children report, 1990

What your money can buy.
   —Save the Children Federation, 1991

One out of five children in the U.S. lacks enough food.
   —*Children 1990: A Report Card, Briefing Book, and Action Primer.* Washington, D.C.: Children's Defense Fund, 1990, pp. 4, 26, 27.

$20 billion per year as the cost to end hunger
   —United Nations Development Report, 1991

   Note: UNICEF says that for $2.5 billion a year **more** than is already being spent, the necessary child survival measures could be put in place to handle those particular problems. The larger $20 billion figure represents the whole picture of substantially ending chronic hunger around the world on a sustainable basis.

Permissions

The authors are grateful to the following individuals and organizations for material used in this book:

- The stories about Osman, Ram, Bimal, Shana, Ellen, and Sebastian were written for *Kids Ending Hunger* by Debra Rein.

- The M&M counting-to-a-billion exercise came from Childreach's See Me, See My World curriculum.

- The height of the tower of a billion kids standing on one another's shoulders came from *How Much Is a Billion?* by David M. Schwartz.

- The recipe for ORS came from the Educator's CARE package, produced by CARE, the international relief and development organization.

- Where Are the Hungry? map came from the Hunger Project, as did the newspaper headline activity.

- The How Many People, How Much Food? activity was adapted from Children Hungering for Justice, Curriculum on Hunger and Children's Rights, from Church World Service's Office of Global Education.

- Close your eyes and imagine a hungry family activity was adapted from Robert Heilbroner, *The Great Ascent*, Harper & Row, 1983.

- The arm band is reproduced by kind permission from The Growth Chart, a tool for use in infant and child health care. Geneva, World Health Organization, 1986.

Special Ending-Hunger Words

Here are some of the special words we used in this book, all collected in one place, in case you forget.

Billion, million A billion (1,000,000,000) is a thousand millions. A million (1,000,000) is a thousand thousands.

Child Survival The work that is saving millions of kids' lives by keeping them from suffering hunger and from catching diseases that kill them.

Chronic hunger When people are getting too little food, or too little of the right kind of food. They may look normal, not as though they are starving. But their bodies are not as strong as they need to be, so the children, especially, die when they catch colds or other sicknesses.

Convention on the Rights of the Child Like a "Bill of Rights" for children. What the United Nations adopted (agreed to) as the civil, economic, social, cultural, and political rights of children. It includes children's survival, development, and protection.

Dehydration Loss of a lot of water from the body, often from diarrhea. Unless something is done, it can and does cause death.

Development Working with the people in a country to help them take care of their problems and improve their lives.

Famine An emergency when a large number of people don't have food and many die.

GOBI	The word to help remember the things that can save millions of the world's children, The letters stand for *Growth* monitoring, *O*ral rehydratrion salts, *B*reast feeding, and *I*mmunization.
Hunger	Not having enough of the kinds of food that help a person to be healthy.
Immunization	A shot that protects the body from diseases such as measles, polio, diphtheria, whooping cough, tetanus, and tuberculosis. Children under five should be immunized so they won't catch the diseases.
Infant mortality rate	The number of babies out of a thousand who die before they are one year old.
ORS (oral rehydration salts)	A very inexpensive mixture of sugar + salt + water that parents can use to treat their children's dehydration from diarrhea.
Ratify	Officially agree to make something become law.
Relief	Taking care of people's immediate health or food or shelter needs. Also called "aid."
World Summit for Children	A meeting of world leaders held in 1990 where they promised to take specific actions to care for the children of the world.

Afterword and Acknowledgments

A Message from Sage

It makes me sad to think about the little children, when they are not healthy or happy and they don't get what they need.

Forty thousand kids die every day. I don't think that it's fair. I think that hunger can be ended. I want it to end, and if other people want it to, then it can be ended faster. That's why we are writing the book—so that other people will want it ended. Then we can figure out a way to get it ended.

I think this is very important. On a scale of 1 to 100, I think it's 100.

People think "Oh, there's nothing we can do about it. It's their problem—they should figure out a way to help themselves."

I think that all the kids and grown-ups should get to have a life like us and should be happy. I don't think we should leave it for other people.

People who have money should give it to plant corn and rice and make roads and give them clothes.

Kids can give other kids life and love. We can let them know that we care.

A Message from Tracy

In 1980 I traveled to Somalia, in East Africa, during a time of bad famine.

Our group visited a refugee camp for the famine victims in the middle of a desert.

There were 70,000 people in that camp. And they were starving.

The only thing that had kept them alive was some bags of food that had been sent by people in countries like yours and mine. The food was running out; if another shipment did not arrive within several days, the whole camp would die.

The water source for all 70,000 people was a hole dug in the sand. What had once been a well was now a muddy pit on its way to drying up.

The only good thing about the situation was the people. The children were weaker than you and your friends, but they still played catch with a ball someone had made by tying rags together, and the boys were still teasing the girls. They thought we looked and sounded very strange, with our funny clothes and language. They circled us and smiled at us.

It was very frightening to think about what was going to happen to all those people. I started to feel terrible that we had not brought food or supplies to give them.

Finally a woman came up to me, walking slowly, with dignity. I was crying, she was not.

She asked, "Why have you come?" I told her through a translator that we had not brought food, but that we had come to find out about the problem and we would go back to our richer countries. I promised that we would tell the world what was happening, that we would ask people to send food right away, and that we would let the world know about hunger, and what they can do, and must do, to end hunger.

She looked into my eyes, and smiled gently. "Yes, yes. Please, then—go quickly." And she walked silently away.

This book is part of my promise to her, to the 70,000 people close to death in that refugee camp, and to the 40,000 children who died yesterday, the day before, and who will continue to die unless we let our love for them inspire us to end hunger, once and for all, forever.

One More Thing...

One thing we haven't mentioned, which is sometimes a little delicate to talk about in public, is what about praying?

In the United States in particular, we like to make sure that all people have the freedom to follow any religion they want—or none at all. So maybe you are a Buddhist or a Christian or a Moslem or a Jew or an atheist or whatever.

However, since this is really a life-and-death matter, it would be great if you included ending hunger in your prayers, or whatever you do when something is really important to you.

If you are a person who doesn't pray, you may want to keep the world's hungry children in your heart and thoughts. Be their protector, their champion, their voice, their friend.

And as you grow up, keep true to your commitment.

*The most exciting part is now ahead...what are **you** going to do?*

In all the world there is no other person quite like you—with your interests, your friends, your family, your ideas!

***You** can change the world—we know you can.*

Tracy and Sage

PS: *Please write to us and let us know any great ideas*
        you come up with, or things you do that really
        work. We'd love to hear what happens when kids
        get into action ending hunger!

        Write to us at:

> Tracy and Sage Howard
> Kids Ending Hunger
> c/o Andrews and McMeel
> 4900 Main St.
> Kansas City, MO 64112

Tribute

This book was made possible by donations

from the following children,

along with their families,

as an expression of their commitment

to a world in which there are

no hungry children.

Koharu, Satsuki, and Sakura Nomura

Daniel, Linus, Matilda, and Anna Jarl

Jonah and Winston Friedman

Christine and William Curtis

Billy, Summer, and Zachary Twist

Kane and Kennedy Kanagawa

Robert Blumenthal

Rachel Erin Greenspan

Rebecca and Andy Mason

Ellen and Valerie Love

Oliver Paul Goddu

Suzanne Marie Parrish

Eli Kutler

Alison and Bobby Huff

Kathryn and Geoffrey Bangs

Sage and Sebastian Howard

Jessica Goldstein

Alexandra Leigh Granat

Elysee S. and Claire M. Ngoi Tshilombo

Rachel and Jesse Solomon

Ari Elegante-Newman

Tagir Saidhoujine

Anton and Rosena Goldman

Maximilian Arion Brossy

Chelsea Lytle

Lucinda Margaret Watson

Christine, Joseph, William, and Matthew Donahue

Joleen Mayu and Sasha Sae Asada

Cristina Harper Cacciotti

Benjamin Rafael and Raúl Sigmund Juliá

Acknowledgments

This book was once an idea only.

The people mentioned below helped turn the idea into the book you are holding in your hands.

We thank them profoundly for their support, and for our shared commitment to the end of hunger.

Many thanks to Mr. Shingo Nomura, who generously provided a grant during the writing and researching of this book.

Then there was The Team: Jean Goldman, whose ownership of the project from the beginning made it all possible; Maria Aycrigg, a one-woman research department; Debra Rein, whose vision and expertise contributed hugely to the manuscript, as do her captivating stories; and Steve Blumenthal, who lovingly and generously contributed his editing skills, his knowledge of the issue of hunger, and his boundless love for and insight into kids.

Also:

Joe Friedman

Allan Henderson

Ted Howard

Diane Wiltshire Kanagawa

Ngoi Tshilombo, Jr.

Hiroshi Ohuchi

Janet Ohuchi

Dorothy Remington

Koji Asada

Carol Coonrod

Renee Deprey

Larry Flynn

Steven Friedland

Hiroshi Furuya

Joan Holmes

Hal Lockwood

Rosemary Lukens

Kuniko Nezu

Hiroshi Ohira

John Painter

Beryl Reubens

Jacki Reubens

Terry Rostov

Beverly Tangri

Tee Thomas

Basil R. Twist III

Youth Ending Hunger

The Hunger Project Research Department

We offer a special acknowledgment to Rei Anela and Sei Kamalei Ohuchi for reminding us all what an opportunity and gift life is, and to Mina, Kai, and Kaori for showing us what children will be like when hunger is ended.

The day that hunger

is eradicated from the earth,

there will be the greatest

spiritual explosion the world has ever known.

Humanity cannot imagine

the joy that will burst forth

into the world on

the day of that great

revolution.

Spanish poet Federico García Lorca